The Story of the Communist Movement in Canada by Tim Buck
2011 Prism Key Press // www.prismkeypress.com

The Story of the Communist Movement in Canada

Tim Buck

Contents

"I think that the Bolsheviks remind us of the hero or Greek mythology, Antænus. They, like Antænus, are strong because they maintain connection with their mother, the masses, who gave birth to them, suckled them and reared them. And as long as they maintain connection with their mother, with the people, they have every chance of remaining invincible."

Stalin
In "Mastering Bolshevism"

Forward

KARL MARX SAID that his theory "is a scandal and abomination to bourgeoisdom and its doctrinaire professors." The Canadian party of Marxism-Leninism for thirty years has abominated the capitalist system which is ravishing our country and selling it as a commodity to U.S. imperialism.

That is its rightful claim to the respect of hundreds of thousands of Canadians, soon to be numbered in millions.

When you read this book, ask yourself the question: "If it were not for the Communists, whence would have come the challenge to economic crisis, fascism, war, unemployment and cultural oppression?" To ask is to answer. Only the Party of Communists has consistently fought these abominations of the profit system.

Others may have criticized this or that feature of capitalism. Only the Communists have drawn the logical and consistent conclusions from that criticism – that the working people of Canada must organize to fight the effects of capitalism upon their lives, and that political struggle to achieve a socialist transformation is the only way to remove the cause of these curses. That record is proof of the teaching of Lenin that only a party of a new type, a Party of Communists, can give leadership to the spontaneous struggle of the people for a better life.

Tim Buck's book conveys the terribly important lesson that it is not enough to criticize capitalism; one must organize the masses to change Canada. He shows that opinions and ideas must lead, not to frustration and cynicism, but to action.

There is no mystery about this method, no dark and murky plot ting. Whoever runs may read. Karl Marx a century ago pointed out the scientific method when he said that

8

Communist philosophy frightens the capitalists "because it includes in its comprehension an affirmative recognition of the existing state of things, at the same time also the recognition of the negation of that state, of its inevitable breaking up; because it regards every historically developed social form as in fluid movement, and therefore takes into account its transient nature no less than its momentary existence; because it is in its essence critical and revolutionary."

This thought may not at first be easy for a worker to grasp, but the struggle to grasp it is part of the education of those who would educate and lead the masses. Tim Buck, better than any Canadian worker, has grasped and put into practice this discovery of genius.

Here is the history of the first generation of Canadian Communists and their efforts to apply this revolutionary concept to our country. It is a history full of drama and struggle. If the bearers of this scientific theory of social change make errors, as they must, it is part of the Marxist method to be obligated to recognize these errors through criticism and self-criticism, in order to correct them as quickly as possible and so to enrich experience and bring understanding closer to reality.

It is a book of struggle. As Beethoven said of his music, politics is its theme – not the shabby dishonesties of capitalist politicians but the struggle to raise the political consciousness of the Canadian workers as they learn by experience the laws of the development of our country.

It is a book of hope for the future. No other party holds out hope for Canada. All the counsels of others lead to despair. There are no greater optimists than the Communists.

Tim Buck's new book enriches a growing library of history of our labor movement. It should be read with A. E. Smith's *All My Life*, Tom McEwen's *He Wrote For Us*, and Tim Buck's older book, *Canada: The Communist Viewpoint*. Soon will be published for the first time a *People's History of Canada*. This scholarship and culture are heralds of the growing maturity of the Canadian working class.

I am confident that when the next chapters of this living history are written, first in action, then in ink, Canada will have started to build socialism. No Canadian will have inspired and led this magnificent march to Communism more than Tim Buck.

–LESLIE MORRIS.

Introduction

THE MODERN working-class movement developed In Canada, as in other capitalist countries, as a direct result of the development of capitalist industry. The first trade union to challenge an employer was that of a group of Toronto printers demanding shorter hours, higher wages and better working conditions, in 1824. They met in an apple orchard at about the spot now known as the Allan Gardens. Since then, trade unionism has developed wherever workers are employed for wages. Its growth and activities have reflected the growth and growing monopolization of Canadian industry.

It was not until the 1870's that the working-class movement undertook large-scale political action. Then, partly under the pressure of similar movements in Britain and the United States, "nine-hour-day leagues" sprang up in industrial centres from the city of Quebec westward to London, Ontario. Through their nine-hour-day movement, workers developed the struggle for legal acknowledgment of the status and rights of the trade union movement. The Trades Union Act of 1873 mirrored the fact that the working class was becoming a factor in the political life of Canada.

With the development of capitalist industry there emerged in Canada, as in the United States, the Populist movement, Knights of Labor, continent-wide craft unions and their federation (the A.F.L,). Expansion of capitalist industry in the 1890's brought a rapid growth of socialist parties.

Canadian workers learned about the class struggle in the course of their own efforts to organize for self-protection. In the 1870's the capitalist class sought to suppress the nine-hour-day movement by arrests of workers' spokesmen and outlawing by court edicts of any actions calculated to cause workers to refrain from work, or to organize the employees of any establishment with a view to collective action against their employer. Adoption of the Trades Union Act did not stop capitalist attempts to suppress the working-class movement; on the contrary, as the working-class movement grew stronger, so capitalist attempts to suppress it became more unscrupulous. An example of the lengths to which the employers went was provided in the report of the "Royal Commission on Industrial Disputes in the Province of British Columbia" in 1903. The report was written by the late Prime Minister W. L. Mackenzie King, then an employee of the Department of Labor. It describes the means by which railway companies planted their agents in the trade union movement, bribed union officials, provoked violence to provide an excuse for the open use of state power. It shows how, by bribery, intimidation, the planting of company agents and provocation, employers undermined and often disrupted the workers' organizations. Jim MacLachlan, the fighting leader of the miners of Nova Scotia, used to illustrate the employers' methods with numerous examples of which the following is typical.

Shortly after the great strike in 1909, two men were killed in a miners' meeting. Those two, along with several others, had been loaded with rum and sent to the meeting with instructions to break it up. In their efforts at disruption they got into a clash with the secretary of the local. A fist fight developed, the secretary pulled a gun and shot the two men dead. He was arrested and charged with murder, but quickly released. Evidence which ultimately came out revealed that the two miners whom he had shot were in the pay of the coal company, had been supplied with rum by coal company officials before being sent to the union meeting, and that the secretary who shot them was an outside operator sent in by a detective agency engaged by the coal company. He didn't know that the two disrupters were company men and they evidently didn't know that he was "one of them." It was one case in which capitalist mistrust of its own undercover operatives led to exposure of the whole corrupt system.

It was in such conditions that the Canadian Marxist movement first developed nation-wide organization. There were Canadian circles of the First International and the continuity of Marxism in our country was illustrated by the fact that among the workers who were associated with the beginnings of the Communist Party of Canada were two who had been members of the First International. It would be erroneous, however, to suggest that the development of Marxism proceeded in a continuous upward line. It crystallized in national organization slowly, due to the colonial isolation of the different provinces and the local character of industry. During the 1890's, however, with the upsurge of industry and the opening up of the West, working-class recognition of Marxism developed rapidly. The Socialist Leagues established in Ontario during the 90's spread through the West to Vancouver Island. With the clarification of political ideas and growing understanding of the need for a fundamental change in the social relations of production, the Socialist Leagues were supplanted by the Socialist Party of Canada. Founded as the Socialist Party of British Columbia, the S.P.C. became a Dominion-wide party in 1904 and achieved organization in five provinces with locals on both Atlantic and Pacific coasts. Canadian locals of the Socialist Labor Party spread into Canada from the United States and numerous local independent labor parties sprang up. Canadian contacts with the labor and socialist movements of other countries were important factors in the spread of socialist activity during that period, in addition to the rapid industrialization of the country.

That same period witnessed the rise of the syndicalist tendency which became such an important influence in the trade union movement of Canada during the first twenty-five years of this century. North American syndicalism combined the influence of the then revolutionary syndicalists in Europe with revolt against the rank conservatism of the leaders of the socalled international unions, particularly the American Federation of Labor, and with elements of petty-bourgeois radicalism inherited

13

from the Knights of Labor which had flourished in the 80's. North American syndicalism attained its full development in the "Industrial Workers of the World." At the height of its strength, from 1911 to 1921, the I.W.W. had organizations in several cities in Canada and a large number of cities in the U.S. With very few exceptions its organizations in cities were very small—propagandist groups rather than unions. Its mass influence was mainly among migratory workers employed in construction, logging, agriculture, etc., who were largely isolated from the weak craft union movement.

The leftist sectarianism of the North American syndicalists and their opportunistic reliance upon spontaneity illustrated the conflict between growing class consciousness and the persisting domination of bourgeois ideas throughout a generation. Due to specific circumstances of economic development, the workers of Canada and the U.S. were very definitely a class by themselves, bound in servitude to monopoly-capital by their complete dependence upon wages, for a long time before any broad strata of them recognized the distinct class interests, needs and historical responsibilities, the struggle for which makes the proletariat a class for itself. The syndicalists advocated economic action exclusively, repudiating the idea of political action. Their "theoreticians" spoke grandiloquently about "revolution by the tactic of folded arms." One result was that social-democratic opportunists of the worst sort enjoyed an almost complete monopoly of labor political support wherever syndicalism had strength. Another was the self-isolation of militants from the majority of organized workers. Correctly condemning the policies of the leaders of the craft unions, they quite wrongly attributed responsibility for those anti-working-class policies to the craft union form. Instead of fighting within the craft unions for progressive policies, for the idea of industrial unionism, for organization of the workers in the great mass-production industries, for the election of leaderships that would express and lead struggles for the class interests and aspirations of the membership, they denounced the craft unions as such, describing them as "job trusts." They called upon militant workers to leave the craft unions, to join their "revolutionary industrial organizations." Their "ideal" unions, with imposing names and small membership, were rarely strong enough to go out and organize workers in the great mass-production industries; most of their energies were expended in fostering secession from the A.F.L. The extreme example of that short-sighted and reckless practice was, in Canada, the One Big Union. The O.B.U. was established by a mass breakaway from the A.F.L. unions in 1919. As long as it existed as a general union, it was dependent upon anti-A.F.L. secessionist sentiment. Cultivation of that sentiment was its main activity.

The syndicalists fought some militant strikes in the United States and Canada; indeed, the Western Federation of Miners was led by syndicalists and expressed syndicalist ideology throughout the most glorious period of its history. More important than the spectacular big strikes, however, were the almost innumerable "job actions" in which individuals or small groups of militant syndicalists led their fellow-workers in wresting gains from the bosses. But the aggressive sectarianism of the I.W.W. and the O.B.U. and other such organizations, their self-isolation from the masses of the workers, their demagogic, counter-revolutionary hostility to the Soviet Union made them, objectively, an anti-working-class force.

During the first fifteen years of the present century the socialist movement in Canada went through an inner development very similar to the development in the socialist parties of Europe during that same period. The striving for political maturity impelled thinking militant members of the movement to fight against opportunist efforts to supplant the struggle for socialism by activity directed solely to social reforms. In the course of the struggle against opportunism they advanced beyond the dogmatic, mechanistic interpretation of Marxism which characterized the Socialist Party of Canada.

The world imperialist war of 1914-1918 signalized the beginning of the breakdown of capitalism and the transition to socialist society. The epoch of the transition to socialism was ushered in with a crash by the great Russian Revolution. The cheers of the workers storming the Winter Palace in far-away Petrograd were echoed in the hearts of hundreds of thousands of Canadian workers. The proclamation by the All-Russian Congress of Workers', Soldiers' and Peasants' Deputies that it was taking over state power was hailed by Canadian workers as an augury of their own historic class role. Broad masses of workers were stirred to their depths. With the end of the imperialist war, the inspirational effect of the Russian Revolution combined with all the pent-up contradictions of class interests in Canada to advance the working-class movement by a stage.

The Socialist Party of Canada was literally overwhelmed by those historic changes. It was true to the teachings of Marx as its leaders understood them but they were enslaved by a narrow, deterministic concept that was essentially anti-Marxist–denying the dynamic revolutionary essence of Marxism. Their propaganda denied the subjective role of the working class in social change. Their attitude toward the trade union movement was disdainful. They sneered at wage struggles as part of the "commodity struggle" of capitalism. They had a supercilious attitude toward parliament and the provincial legislatures also, but many leading members of the S.P.C. were trade union officials and contested parliamentary elections. A few of them got elected. Let it be added that most of them utilized their election campaigns to popularize Marxism as they understood it. For example, Charlie O'Brien, elected to the Alberta legislature in 1909 by the miners of the Crow's Nest Pass, proclaimed himself a revolutionary socialist in every campaign speech and, wrongly, emphasized almost solely his opinion that the workers could achieve nothing by electing him or anybody else.

The contradictions between their verbal contempt for the daily struggles of the workers and their desire for trade union

16

office and seats in elected assemblies was never resolved by the leaders of the S.P.C.; indeed, they never showed recognition of the need to resolve it, Their mechanical, deterministic conception of the science of Marxism is illustrated by the following key sentence in their manifesto greeting the great Russian Revolution.

"If they have sinned against the Holy Ghost by revolting before the evolutionary alarm clock called them, we freely forgive them, and humbly hope that those who await the appointed hour will bear themselves as valiantly."[1]

Continuing that attitude, a member of the executive of the S.P.C. who became editor of its official organ assured its diminishing membership in 1922: "While we don't seem to be making much progress we are in tune with the infinite."

A year later one of the outstanding "theoreticians" of the S.P.C. wrote that: "From the prophetic teaching of capitalism's collapse we have passed back to a period void and empty of any revolutionary outlook." Those statements characterized the attitude of the "leaders" of the Socialist Party of Canada during the years immediately following the First World War and the Russian Revolution. It was not surprising that they ended their pretence at Marxism disgracefully, echoing the capitalist lie that fascism is evoked by "Communist force and violence."

Against the dogmatic passivity and anti-working-class snobbery of the Socialist Party, there developed a revolt that was expressed in two distinct tendencies. One, which developed within locals of the S.P.C. itself, was typified by the establishment of the Socialist Party of North America. The S.P.N.A. emphasized the importance of merging Marxist theory with the daily struggles of the working class. It required every member of the party to be a member of the union in his or her place of work and to submit to examination by his fellow-S.N.P.A. members of his understanding of the three fundamentals of Marxism-dialectical materialism, surplus value, the class struggle.

The other tendency brought into being the Social Democratic Party of Canada. The S.D.P. was founded in Winnipeg by uniting the local S.D.P. and the Social Democratic Federation of Ontario. The S.D.P. was numerically stronger than the S.P.C.

While the S.D.P. was founded, in the main, upon the European traditions, its role in Canada was markedly different from the role of social democracy in Europe. Workers who had come here from continental Europe made a great contribution to the development of the labor movement in Canada through the building of the S.D.P. They constituted the majority of its membership, its main working force in campaigns and in extending its organization. They won respect for socialist organization by the energy and devotion displayed in their campaigns. An outstanding example is to be seen in the 10,000 votes secured for Comrade Lindala, a Finnish working man who was the social democratic candidate for the Board of Control in the city of Toronto in 1912. The S.D.P. made opportunist mistakes, some of its leaders were very much under the influence of European social democracy, but its membership included the most militant sections of the Canadian working class, giving courageous and energetic support to labor in every struggle.

The first public action looking to the foundation of a Communist Party of Canada originated in the S.D.P. when Comrade Niznevitch, secretary of the Toronto organization, sent out a circular in January, 1919, inviting attendance at a conference to consider the need for a new revolutionary party. Contrary to the social democratic parties in Europe, the weight of opinion within the S.D.P. of Canada was so strongly in favor of the left that after the founding of the Communist Party of Canada there was no national social democratic party in Canada again until the C.C.F. was organized in 1933.

Thus, when the First World War broke out Marxism was already a national force in Canada. The support of class-conscious workers was competed for by organizations representing three main trends, typified by the Socialist Party of Canada the Social Democratic Party of Canada and the Socialist Party of North America. The numerous local independent labor parties, the Canadian locals of the Socialist Labor Party, each corresponded politically with one or another of these three currents of socialist activity.

During 1918 there was a rapid growth of trade union organization and of working-class political activity. The majority of Canadian workers sympathized with the workers and peasants who had taken over what had been the empire of the tsars, "the prison-house of nations." They recognized the imperialist attempts to overthrow the Soviet government by military intervention as an attack upon the working class as a whole. The Western Labor Conference held in Calgary in March, 1919, sent messages of solidarity to Lenin, to the Soviet government and to the Red Army. It telegraphed the Canadian government demanding the withdrawal of Canadian forces and an end to imperialist intervention in Soviet Russia. In May, 1919, the great Winnipeg Strike started, first as a strike of the metal trades workers, extending rapidly to a general sympathetic strike of all the workers in the city. The Winnipeg General Strike was a strike of craft unions, but it was trade union action at a very high level. The Strike Committee became in a large measure responsible for the whole community. Bread was baked, milk was delivered to hospitals, the city power plants and waterworks were operated–for a while even the municipal police did duty–solely by the decision of the Strike Committee. In spite of the fact that the organizers of the strike were not prepared for the responsibilities that they were called upon to meet, elements of workers' power developed. Public order was complete until the capitalists resorted to violence with their so-called "Committee of One Thousand." When the capitalists and their dupes resorted to violence, they could not have succeeded alone. To break that strike, Canadian capitalism through its coalition Tory-Liberal government resorted to state violence in defiance Of its own laws. When the minister of labor, Gideon Robertson, vice-president of an international union, telegraphed the prime minister that there were no legal grounds upon which the strike leaders could be arrested, Arthur Meighen replied, III effect: arrest them anyway, I will write a law afterwards to legalize your action. The leaders of the strike were taken from their beds in nocturnal police raids, spirited out of Winnipeg and held incommunicado until the strike was broken. Meighen "legalized" the outrage by an order-in-council which, later, was elaborated to become the infamous Section 98 of the Criminal Code.

Working-class pride in the solidarity of the workers of Winnipeg could not blind Canadian Marxists to the fact that the ideas represented by Its leaders were wrong. As more and more of Lenin's writings were translated, it became obvious to most of us that the line of policy fought for by the S.P.N.A. was more in accord with the teachings of Lenin than were either the dogmatic assertion of orthodoxy which screened the sectarian passivity of the Socialist Party of Canada or the syndicalist confusion and political sterility of the I.W.W. and the O.B.U. Simultaneously, the left-wing activists of the Social Democratic Party recognized through Lenin's teachings the necessity for unification of all revolutionary workers in one party. By the summer of 1920 we secured our first copies of the *Theses and Statutes* from Washington. The U.S. government had them translated and printed in a handy pamphlet, as part of its anti-Soviet campaign.

There was already a widespread recognition of the necessity for the unification of the Left in a party of a new type, the Communist Party. It was out of that working-class unity of purpose–not out of the fantastic schemes conjured up in the distorted imaginations of the Colonel Drews, the Maurice Duplessis', and the servile hacks of the capitalist press, that the Communist Party of Canada was born.

20

Note

1. Manifesto of the Socialist Party of Canada, 5th Edition, p. 2.

CHAPTER ONE: A Party of a New Type

BEFORE the Communist Party of Canada was founded many left-wingers had already become members of either the Communist Party of America, or the United Communist Party of America. Each of those parties had set up Canadian districts. It was clear to Canadian members of both parties that Communist unity in an independent Canadian party was a primary need. In 1920 there was widespread discussion between the various groups, looking to unity. A joint committee was set up, aiming at unity of the Canadian districts of the C.P.A. and the U.C.P.A. In June, 1921, a unity convention was held and for the first time all the workers organized in Canada under the banner of Marx and Lenin were united in one party: The Communist Party of Canada.

The War Measures Act still outlawed revolutionary working-class organizations. The unity conference had to be held in utmost secrecy, in a barn on the outskirts of Guelph, Ontario. Founded in conditions of illegality, our party started as an underground organization. The problem of public activity and mass connections with the workers confronted the leadership from the beginning. The imperative need to solve that problem was emphasized particularly by the Third World Congress of the Communist International, held during July and August of that year. The C.I. called upon Communists everywhere to unite the working class in broad popular activities. After consultation with active left-wingers in various parts of the country, a conference was convened in Toronto, December 11 and 12, 1921, to consider the launching of a public working-class party based upon the theses and statutes of the Communist International. There was universal agreement upon the necessity for such a party.

The conference adopted a five-point provisional platform, setting forth the aims to which the delegates considered the new party should dedicate itself, under the following heads:

1. *For a Workers' Republic*
"... the alternative to the capitalist system is a working-class government. The Workers' Party shall lead the workers in struggle towards the establishment of the Workers' Republic of Canada."

2. *Working-Class Political Action*
"... The Workers' Party shall take part, whenever possible, in all such campaigns ... so that ultimately the real issue will be laid clear, and we, the working class, shall eventually triumph at the expense of the enemies of the working class, the capitalist oppressors."

3. *Trade Union Unity*
"To help educate trade unionists to appreciate the possibilities of their organizations as definite factors in carrying on the class battles caused by capitalist oppression, to initiate a movement to expose the tyranny and treachery of the reactionary labor bureaucrats, and to make the unions real fighting working-class units."

4. *A Party of Action*
"The party shall be composed of militant, class-conscious workers, members shall be subject to the discipline of the party and the direction of the national executive committee, which shall be the highest expression of the party between conventions. Democratic centralization shall be the guiding organizational principle of the Workers' Party...."

5. *A Party Press*
"The party shall eventually acquire a party press in order to give expression to the interests and aims of the working-class movement...."

The delegates addressed a manifesto "To the Workers of Canada" typified by the following excerpts:

"We address our manifesto to all workers. We cannot sit down and wait patiently for capitalism to collapse. Conditions call for fight, for action. With the prospects of further unemployment, a more intensified open-shop campaign and, in the near future, imperialist war, the Workers' Party of Canada issues this call. If we are to survive we must be free from capitalist domination. If the capitalist class is to dominate we must suffer even more bitterly.

"The issue is clear, therefore, between unemployment and prosperity, organized tyranny and political freedom, capitalist state and workers' republic.

"Working men and working women! We call upon you to play your parts in the establishment of a real live working-class party which shall ultimately produce a fighting machine able to organize and direct the oppressed masses in their struggles for political and economic freedom. Rally to the call for complete emancipation! In answer to the oppression of the capitalist class let our battle cry be:

'Workers of the World Unite! You have nothing to lose but your chains of wage slavery! You have a World to Gain!'"

A provisional national committee was elected, charged with the task of organizing a constituent convention. At that convention, held on February 22-23, attended by delegates representing organizations in six provinces,[1] a legal Communist party, the Workers' Party of Canada, was established.[2]

The prominent differences between the radicals at that time were illustrated by the fact that the issue which evoked keenest debate and the only organizational defection in the constituent convention was not the "new" issue of the dictatorship of the proletariat but whether the Workers' Party would make secession from the conservative unions its labor union tactic and the One Big Union its "industrial arm." Enslaved by the idea that secession from the craft unions was the hallmark of militancy, the delegates of the One Big Union demanded of the convention that the new party declare war upon the A.F.L. and, indeed, upon all craft unions. The convention rejected that

24

demand. Guided by the lessons that Lenin had emphasized in his recently translated *Left-Wing Communism*, it called upon members of the new party to join the unions that were supported by the masses of the workers in their industries and to fight there for genuine working-class policies.

By maintaining the unity of Communist organization while rejecting the long-established practice of war against the craft unions, the constituent convention took the first great stride toward making Marxism-Leninism a force for the unification and the political development of the Canadian working class.

The Workers' Party was qualitatively superior to all of the various parties that had preceded it. It was historically superior in that it based its theory and practice upon Lenin's fundamental re-clarification of the teachings of Marx and Engels on, the state, on the subjective role of the revolutionary proletariat, and on the character of the state in the transition from capitalism to communism. As noted above, the organizational principle of the Workers' Party was democratic centralism. Out of those fundamental differences there developed marked differences on numerous questions. The Workers' Party dedicated itself to the task of helping the proletariat to become a class *for* itself. In contrast to the Socialist Party of Canada, it emphasized the necessity for the development of broad popular campaigns around the issues of the day, directed to strengthening the workers' understanding of their role as a class. In contrast to the S.P.C., with its contempt for the workers' economic struggles, the Workers' Party sought to unite Marxist theory with correct working-class practice in consistent and devoted support of all such struggles. The educational campaign carried on by the Workers' Party (later the Communist Party) through the 1920's, to develop widespread understanding among the workers of how modern industry was making industrial unionism necessary, was one of its great contributions to the Canadian labor movement. In combination with its systematic propaganda for industrial unionism, the Workers' Party developed its great "back-to-the unions" campaign and made the slogan "No struggle too small, no struggle too large" a law of party practice. In marked contrast to the general, all too general, propaganda which had been the sole Marxist activity of the socialist parties which had preceded it, the Workers' Party emphasized the necessity for systematic, organized struggle and study around every issue of working-class interest as an organic part of the long-term struggle for socialism. Against the false and anti-Marxist subservience to working-class "spontaneity" that had characterized the attitude of the syndicalists and previous socialist parties, the Workers' Party exposed subservience to spontaneity as one of the main sources of opportunism in the labor movement. It placed primary emphasis, for the first time in Canada, upon the study of theory "as a guide to action."

The main resolutions adopted by the constituent convention illustrated the character of the new party. For the first time in the history of socialism in Canada, a revolutionary workers' party, dedicated to the struggle for socialism, called upon all radical workers to join the unions which commanded the support of the great majority of the organized workers and to fight for their upbuilding and unification. Here, for the first time, a revolutionary party called for the building of a labor party and for farmer-labor unity in all-sided struggle against big capital.

Next to defining the role that it aimed to play and the policies for which it would fight, the main task of the party following the constituent convention was establishment of its press. It should be mentioned here that the labor press, though weak, had a well-established tradition in Canada. The provisional conference which had started the movement to establish the Workers' Party had been convened on the initiative of *The Workers' Guard*, published under the direction of the underground Communist Party, edited at that time by Fred Peel, a foundation member of the party. Other influential papers such as the *B.C. Federationist* (British Columbia), *The Maritime Labor Herald* (Nova Scotia), *The New Democracy* (Hamilton, Ontario) , and several weeklies published in languages other than English, gave support to the policies of the Communist International in varying degrees. Following the unity convention in June, 1921, the Central Committee of the Communist Party of Canada initiated *The Communist*, a four-page paper in newspaper format. Because of lack of resources and the difficulty of distribution, only four issues were published.

However, there had not yet been published a legal periodical which was the official voice and collective organizer of the Communist movement . Such a paper was established with the founding of *The Worker*, the first issue of which appeared March 15, 1922.

The establishment of a legal official organ of the Communist movement opened a new era for the working-class press in Canada. At the beginning, *The Worker* was published only twice a month. Its editor was a law student attending Toronto University. It was transformed into a weekly after its fourth or fifth issue when a delegation requested an interview with two officers of the party[3] to inform them that immigrant workers in Toronto had decided to raise $100 a week for *The Worker* every week until the next party convention.

That inspiring demonstration of proletarian solidarity was consistent with the tradition that the advanced detachments of the workers from Europe had already established in the working-class movement. It should be mentioned that among the founders of the Workers' Party there were several who had already felt the ruthless hand of capitalist justice in the service of the capitalist class. John Boychuk, Tom Bell, Mrs. Custance and others had been arrested early in 1919 under the authority of the War Measures Act. Their "crime" had been that of attending a conference for the purpose of establishing an International Workers Association to unite workers in support of the Russian Revolution and to further the struggle for socialism in Canada. Tom Bell and John Boychuk had been sentenced to prison terms. John Boychuk was released only a few months before our constituent convention. Among those who were leading members of our party during those early years, names which personified the national groups and the democratic organizations built by immigrant workers ranked very high. During the early period of struggle against secession as the labor union tactic of revolutionary workers and for a mass "back-to-the-unions" movement, immigrant workers from Europe led the way. Later immigrant workers shouldered a very large share of the struggles and sacrifices that went into the building of industrial unions by the Workers' Unity League and the C.I.O. Their lives–in the majority of cases their children's lives also–are expended in building Canada. Their only hope for happiness and a modicum of physical well-being lies in winning these things for all Canadians. They have enriched our movement and Canada as a whole by their contributions on the picket line, in the building of organizations and in their enrichment of our culture. Their underwriting of the party's English-language press in 1922 typified the role of which democratic members of the national groups are justly proud.

The popular issues confronting the working-class movement in 1922 differed from the issues of today. Canada's relationship to the United Kingdom was still one of constitutional inferiority. A very influential section of the Canadian bourgeoisie wanted to maintain that relationship. Arthur Meighen, the national leader of the Conservative Party, was urging the establishment of a supra-national "Imperial Cabinet." Another section, personified by Sir Clifford Sifton, advocated an assertion of Canada's independence by a direct change in the constitution. Under the influence of United States imperialism, a majority of the bourgeoisie arrived at support of Mackenzie King's technique of leaving the B.N.A. Act alone, while asserting Canadian sovereignty from case to case as the need arose and their interests demanded.

While not yet fully understanding the devious ways of the Canadian bourgeoisie and their new prime minister, Mackenzie

King, the Workers' Party correctly called upon the labor movement to take a stand for "Canadian Independence." For the first time in Canadian history the party of the revolutionary workers pledged itself to the struggle for national sovereignty.

While grasping the significance of Lenin's emphasis upon the role of the working class in the struggle to protect the real interests of the nation, the party did not then grasp the full historical significance of the national status of the people of French Canada and therefore failed to put forward the necessary demand for the right of the people of French Canada to national self-determination up to the right of secession. During the first year following the foundation of the Workers' Party, there was established a French section under the leadership of the very well-known anarcho-communist of Montreal, St. Martin. The group had operated for some time as "l'Université Ouvrier." Under St. Martin's leadership they had applied directly to the Communist International for affiliation as the Communist Party of Canada. The executive of the Communist International had urged unity of all Canadian adherents of the International in one party and the group affiliated to the Workers' Party as the French section. Unfortunately, the attitude of St. Martin combined the political weaknesses which had characterized both the right wing of the Socialist Party of Canada and the syndicalists, with extreme petty-bourgeois nationalism. He was violently opposed to any worker joining the international unions. He was violently and demonstratively anti-clerical but he differentiated between the international craft unions and the Catholic Syndicates on the ground that the latter were "Quebecois."[4] At the same time his attitude towards the national problem of French Canada and its people was one of national nihilism. The majority of the members of what became the French section of the Workers' Party of Canada were honest revolutionary workers. Several of them, personified by Elphege Paquette, were and continued to be throughout their lives, loyal adherents of the revolutionary ideas of Marx and Lenin. But the majority of the members were completely under the ideological domination of St. Martin. The result was that the orgnization failed to take up the issues that were of fundamental concern to the workers and farmers of Quebec. It stagnated in sectarian isolation from the masses, a barrier between communism and the workers of French Canada until the great economic crisis overwhelmed even the sectarianism of St. Martin. Then a group of workers headed by Evariste Dube broke from the St. Martin tradition and, guided by Fred Rose, made the Communist movement an organic part of the mass activit of the working class in French Canada.

In the field of trade union activity the party supported the program and the organized activity of the Trade Union Educational League. The program of action of the Canadian section of the T.U.E.L. was as follows:[5]

1. Organize the Unorganized Workers for Higher Wages, Shorter Hours.
2. Organize a Powerful Minority Movement Within the Trade Unions.
3. Organize Shop Committees.
4. United Independent Labor Political Action.
5. Canadian Trade Union Autonomy.
6. Affiliation of Every Functioning Trade Union to the Trades and Labor Congress of Canada.
7. Affiliation of Every Local Union to the Local Trades and Labour Councils.
8. Build a Workers' Press.
9. Nationalization of Industry.
10. Amalgamate the Craft Unions.
11. International Trade Union Unity.
12. The Abolition of Capitalism.

Because of the widespread split that had accompanied the establishment of the One Big Union, the first general task that the party set itself was to persuade radical workers to spark a "back-to-the-unions" movement. The Workers' Party was built in the struggle to correct the mistaken worship of secession among Canadian radicals. The party's early organizers were simultaneously the initiators of campaigns to organize the unorganized, to reunite in one union workers who had become divided in the course of the class struggle, etc. They were the most respected advisers on trade union tactics, their meetings were tribunes of the rank and file trade unionists. It was not only the party organizers who had already been identified with the trade union movement for a long time who won that respect. As workers recognized the basic fact that the trade union advice of the Workers' Party was based solely and squarely upon the interests of the working class and not upon a fight for dues, they sought our advice. During that period Annie Buller and Beckle Buhay went into literally every camp in the mining districts of Nova Scotia, Northern Ontario, Alberta and British Columbia; the miners, including thousands who were not members of our party, sought advice from them as eagerly as from Tim Buck. At a later date the same was true of our late beloved comrade Jeanne Corbin in Northern Ontario.

The effects of the campaign to reunite the radicals with the masses of the workers in the old unions provided striking vindications of the labor union policy of the party. All over the country, militant workers who had been sitting on the sidelines returned to the craft unions. Their presence and work was reflected almost immediately in increasing militant trade union action. The campaign of the Trade Union Educational League for trade union unity, its official organ, *The Labor Herald*, and the paper published by its Canadian section, *The Left Wing*, received active support from local unions in every part of the country.

Organizations embracing a third of the trade unionists in Canada endorsed the program of the T.U.E.L. The "back-to-the-unions" campaign transformed the political content of trade union activity. Militancy supplanted passivity over a wide area of the movement. When the regular convention of District 26, United Mine Workers of America, at Truro, Nova Scotia, in June, 1922, was addressed by the Canadian secretary of the T.U.E.L., the delegates endorsed the program by unanimous vote, extended an official invitation to the secretary to visit every local of the union and instructed the officers of the district to apply immediately for affiliation to the Red International of Labor Unions. The miners of Nova Scotia were not the only workers who responded to the T.U.E.L. campaign. Scores of local unions of railways workers supported it, with particular emphasis upon the idea of amalgamating all the craft unions into one great industrial union of railway workers. In Alberta the return of the militants to the United Mine Workers of America brought about a transformation of that union's effectiveness. When the autonomy of the district was restored in 1923 and district elections were held, the entire slate of candidates put forward by the left wing under the leadership of the T.U.E.L. was elected. The miners immediately went out on an organizational campaign to bring back into the union all the open-shop mines, the operators of which had been exploiting the split in the labor movement. Within less than a year more miners were organized than ever before in the history of District 18.

In the field of independent working-class political action the Workers' Party supported the effort to build the Canadian Labor Party. The C.L.P., founded in 1921, while the Trades and Labor Congress was in convention at Winnipeg,[6] was a federated party. Its organizational structure was based upon provincial sections. In every locality all unions and other working-class organizations affiliated to the party co-ordinated their parliamentary activities through a delegate council. Each provincial section was autonomous in provincial matters within the framework established by the national program of the party. Each provincial section held separate annual conventions, the annual national conventions being made up of delegates elected in provincial conventions. The C.L.P. was open to all and any working-class organization. The only conditions were that affiliated organizations should abide by the program and discipline of the C.L.P. in electoral activities and should not at any time engage in anti-working-class activities. The C.L.P. was a working-class political united front. Some marked gains were made during the five years in which its unity was maintained. There is no doubt whatever that its continued development would have made the organized labor movement an important parliamentary force in Canada.

The Workers' Party, for the first time in the history of the revolutionary workers' movement in Canada, recognized the special interests of working-class women and undertook to organize them. The main channel was the Federation of Women's Labor Leagues. These were local organizations of women which took up the fight on every question that concerned the interests or the special needs of women workers, working-class housewives, etc. In those days the minimum wage laws, where they existed, were enforced only by tireless effort. For example, one day a girl employed in a large chocolate factory in the city of Toronto approached Mrs. Florence Custance, the president of the Toronto Women's Labor League, with a request for information as to "how the minimum wage act works." Conversation with the girl led Mrs. Custance to suspect that few of her fellow-workers were getting the minimum wage, supposedly guaranteed by law. Fear of losing her job frightened the girl away even before, she had heard all the information she came for. Pursuing the matter, the local Women's Labor League canvassed the girls of the factory. The eventual result was that eighty of them received substantial wage increases and accumulated back pay. Such activities were carried on everywhere by the Women's Labor Leagues. They were active in elections, in trade union organizing campaigns, in aid to strikers, and they were the first organizers of systematic anti-militarist activities in English Canada. Their "No More War" parades were a high point of labor activities as early as 1923. At the height of its development, the Women's Labor League movement had organizations in twenty-two areas. Their leaders, typified by Mrs. Annie Whitfield in the East, Mrs. Florence

Custance in Central Canada, and Mary English in the West, became the recognized representatives of the progressive working-class women of Canada. Delegates of the W.L.L. were seated on Trades and Labor Councils all across the country.

At the second convention of the Workers' Party, in 1923, delegates representing several local organizations of the revolutionary youth met in constituent convention and established the Young Workers' League of Canada. Leslie Morris of Winnipeg was its first national secretary, A. T. Hill of Finland, Ontario, its first national chairman. The Y.W.L. established local organizations throughout Ontario, in wide areas of Alberta and British Columbia, and in several localities in Saskatchewan and Manitoba. The local organizations already established in Montreal were among the most active in founding the national organization but the Y.W.L. (later the Y.C.L.) made very little headway among the French youth during the early years of its existence.

At its third national convention in 1924, the party changed its name to the Communist Party of Canada. Until then the party had combined federalism with individual membership. Mass organizations could affiliate *en bloc*. With the change of name, that practice was abolished. Since then individual payment of dues has been the sole form of membership. The 1924 convention placed the main emphasis on party activity in the places of work and called upon its members to build shop nuclei. In addition to limiting membership to individuals, the convention added to the constitution a membership obligation and a specific definition of party units. The following was the obligation:

Article 3
SECTION 1: Applicants for membership, shall sign an application card, reading as follows: "I, the undersigned, declare my adherence to the principles and tactics of the Communist Party of Canada, as expressed in the program and constitution, subscribe to the party press, and agree to submit to the discipline of the party, and pledge myself to

engage actively in its work."

Article 4

SECTION 1: The basic units of the Communist Party of Canada shall be factory groups, area units, farm clubs and units based upon a language other than English where necessary.

During 1924-1925 the party started development of systematic municipal activities. The first Communist alderman in North America, Bill Kolysnik, had already been elected in Winnipeg and councillors had been elected in several smaller municipalities. These successes, however, had been achieved in spite of the fact that the party virtually ignored this type of activity. From 1924, recognition of the vital importance of municipal government in the fight for democracy and peace became increasingly evident in the party's work.

In September, 1925, the Toronto party committee convened a meeting at the Labor Temple at 167 Church Street to initiate organized action for the defence of victims of the class war. The immediate purpose of the meeting was to help defend miners who were then committed for trial upon charges arising from the great miners' strikes in Alberta. Tim Buck, who had played a leading role in the strike, gave a first-hand description of conditions in the mining camps, the causes of the strike, the shooting of Bert Renners (shot in mistake for Buck) and the plight of the miners and their families. He called upon the workers of Toronto to demonstrate their solidarity with the miners by providing substantial assistance for the arrested workers and their families, and for the legal defence of those who, like Louis MacDonald and Cecil Boone, might be railroaded to prison for long terms unless the police and courts in the mining districts were made to feel the pressure of democratic working-class support of the miners.

In that meeting there was or anized the Toronto Committee for Labor Defence. Mrs. Florence Custance was elected then and there as secretary. Within a few months a score of similar local organizations were established and the Canadian Labor Defence League was born. Mrs. Custance was its first national secretary. Later, under the joint leadership of Comrades Becky Buhay and our late beloved A. E. Smith, the Canadian Labor Defence League became a great mass movement and played a famous and heroic role.

In its early stages, the party did not yet measure up to the standards established by Lenin, very largely because of the inability of the leaders of the party to free themselves from the sectarian traditions of the revolutionary movement in Canada, and the ideological influence of the bourgeoisie. To overcome those weaknesses, the party membership had to advance politically to the stage at which it demanded leadership of a higher quality. It required a more critical and self-critical attitude on the part of all party members towards the party itself. In the early 1920's we did not yet understand that systematic use of criticism and self-criticism is "the law of growth of communist parties." It took some years of Stalin's patient, persistent teaching to achieve that understanding. But, as shown above, the Workers' Party was a party of a new type. By devoted and unqualified support of every genuine working-class struggle it made its history as a party an inseparable part of the history of the working-class movement as a whole. By the same devoted participation in militant struggles, it earned its title of The Party of the Working Class.

Note

1. Quebec, Ontario, Manitoba, Saskatchewan, Alberta and British Columbia. No organization in the Maritimes was represented but the decisions of the conference received immediate and active support in the Maritimes from active and highly respected spokesmen of the revolutionary groups there: e.g., Jim MacLachlan, Joe Wallace, Roscoe Filmore and Harold Ross, each

of whom spoke publicly in support of the projected new party and organized support for it in their localities.

2. The first Central Committee of the new party was composed of: Bill Moriarty (general secretary), Maurice Spector (editor), Mrs. Florence Custance, Joe Knight, Mrs, Joanna (Johnny) Knight, Tom Bell, Jack MacDonald, Trevor Maguire, Tim Buck, Mike Buhay, Alex Gauld, Jack Margolese, John Boychuk, A. Ahlgvist, J. Latva, A. Green, M. Popovich, J. Navis, J. Penner, Malcolm Bruce, Walter Mills, Jack Lakeman, Bob Mogeridge, Phil Christophers, Jack Kavanagh, Bill Bennett. The first twelve named were all of Toronto. The first nine named constituted the Political Bureau elected by the Central Committee.

3. Bill Moriarty and Tim Buck. The delegation was headed by the late Comrade Ahlqvist, then chairman of the Finnish Organization of Canada.

4. The Catholic Syndicates had not then evolved into genuine labor unions. Under the direction of the church in Quebec they repudiated strike action and "the class struggle" in general.

5. *Steps to Power.* Programmatic pamphlet of the T.U.E.L., 1925.

6. The convention which expelled A. R. Mosher for "dual unionism."

CHAPTER TWO: A Decade of Great Struggles

THE 1920's WAS A period of great militant working-class struggles and, simultaneously, of cunningly engineered anti-working-class schemes by which top trade union leaders sought to transform the unions into part of the "efficiency" machinery of the capitalist class. The Winnipeg General Strike had opened up a period of widespread trade union struggles for wage increases, union recognition and for the right of the workers to establish unions of their own choice. The short-lived, immediate post-war period came to a sudden end with the collapse of the inflationary speculative boom at the end of 1920. The year 1921 was one of crisis. The effect of the crisis was aggravated for the working class by the veritable orgy of mergers and over-capitalization that characterized the operations of finance-capital during that period. The illustrations quoted below are typical.

"Bearing in mind the very close relationship between the banks and the industries of the country, it is interesting to note that during 1922-23-24, 5 of the 18 chartered banks in the Dominion suffered such severe losses through the writing down of investment values as to compel suspension or absorption; while the Union Bank, the fifth largest in Canada, caused a considerable, flurry by transferring over four and a half million dollars from its reserve to cover losses of the same kind, and finally had to be absorbed by the Royal Bank."

"The Amalgamated Asbestos Corp. Ltd. started out with an original capital of $3,550,000. They watered this by $14,450,000 which brought the total paper value of their stock to $18,000,000. That meant that dividends had to be raised for this $14,450,000 in addition to dividends on the actual capital invested."

"Ames Holden-McCready Co. Ltd., at the time of their reorganization, had a capitalization of $3,500,000. $8,000,000 of water was poured into the original stock boosting their paper capitalization up to $11,500,000."

"The Canada Steamship Lines Ltd., when organized by the merger of a number of smaller companies, had a total capital of $16,200,000. They turned the water hose into their stock bucket, and poured in $16,800,000 worth of paper, boosting their paper capitalization up to the enormous level Of $33,000,000."[1]

In the pulp and paper, mining, automobile, and general manufacturing industries, the story was the same. A deep crisis of over-capitalization and sharp contraction of markets beset the entire capitalist system and threatened its beneficiaries with breakdown. Canadian capitalists "dealt" with the crisis by ruthless attacks on the living standards of the working class. They sought to secure the same volume of profits from a lower level of economic activity by more intense exploitation of those workers who were fortunate enough to have jobs, and a highly organized drive against the trade unions. Sparked by an international conference of bankers held in Brussels, Belgium, the manufacturers' associations of the United States and Canada launched a systematic and violent "open-shop" drive. Their proclaimed aim was to "reduce the cost of production." The workers were militant, and resisted; but the reactionary top officialdom of the unions refused to organize united labor opposition to the bosses' open-shop and wage-cutting campaign. Instead they sought to utilize the bosses' offensive to their own advantage. Under the deceitful slogan "clean out the Reds," they launched a vicious campaign within the unions to consolidate their own grip upon them. They expelled militant workers right and left while changing union policies to conciliate the bosses. Under the lying pretence that they were pursuing "the higher strategy of labor," they transformed the unions from organizations for working-class struggle into machinery for anti-working-class collaboration with the bosses—in some industries they made the unions the official agencies through which the bosses enforced man-killing speed-up. The results were disastrous for the workers. The workers in turn lost faith in the international unions and deserted them in disgust. By the end of 1925, their membership in Canada had been reduced to less than a quarter of a million.

As noted earlier, trade union organization was limited, in the main, to the "sheltered trades." The exceptions were coal miners and railway workers. The mass industries—textiles, packing, logging and sawmill workers, furniture workers, general manufacturing, etc.—were unorganized. All the workers suffered ruthless wage cuts and speed-up during that period, including the well-organized railway shopmen and the militant coal miners. Between 1920 and 1926 wages were cut by an average of twenty-two per cent.

The bosses did not achieve their ends without bitter struggle however. In industry after industry the workers fought back against wage cuts. The strikes of the longshoremen in British Columbia, longshoremen and shoe-workers in Quebec, miners in Nova Scotia, Alberta, and British Columbia, metal trades workers, printing trades workers and others in the Toronto area, stopped the wage-cutting offensive far short of the employers' objectives.

Because they were the best organized and the most militant, the resistance of the coal miners to the wage-cutting campaign exemplified the best of those struggles. In Alberta, for example, the miners struck for seven months, from May 1, 1924, against the demand of the Western Colliery Managers' Association for a twenty-two per cent wage cut. The miners finally accepted a ten per cent wage cut, returning to work at the end of the year. Within two months of their return to work Philip Murray, on behalf of the general executive board of the U.M.W.A., signed the "Tri-State[2] Agreement" at Jacksonville,

Florida, abolishing the national wage-scale and opening the way for wage reductions in the mining industry all over the United States and Canada. The Western Colliery Managers' Association demanded equivalent wage reductions, in the Alberta mines. With the tacit agreement of the U.M.W.A. leadership they posted up notices at the pit-heads announcing a further fifteen per cent reduction. The miners fought those reductions. Against the announced policy of the union leadership to supply the operators with other miners if necessary, they struck the mines. The Province of Alberta and the mining towns of eastern British Columbia were torn with bitter struggles throughout 1925, aggravated by the conflict between the overwhelming majority of the rank-and-file miners who wanted to defeat the attempts of the operators to reduce their standard of living, and the official leadership of the U.M.W.A. which accepted the operators' terms and collaborated with them in forcing the miners back into the pits.

The odds against which militant workers had to fight during that period, as well as the very high political level of many of their trade union actions, were exemplified in the continual struggles of the miners and steelworkers in Nova Scotia through 1920-1925. Indeed, their struggles marked the highest level attained by Canadian trade union action up to that time.

Ownership of the province-wide coal mines and steel mills and their ancillary operations had been merged in an octopus named British Empire Steel Corporation (Besco). The miners finally had compelled Besco to recognize their union, the U.M.W.A., after more than ten years of struggle marked by repeated police violence. At last, at the end of November, 1921, the union won from the corporation a basic rate of $5.00 per day for all workers employed underground. In January, 1922, Besco cut the miners' wages again without so much as a pretence at consultation with the union. During the following eighteen months, while the miners' leaders strove doggedly to compel the corporation to negotiate the miners' wage rate, the corporation pressed its offensive against the steelworkers also, combining victimization of active union men with systematic chiselling on wage rates.

Steelworkers earnings had averaged $5.20 per day in 1920, but by the spring of 1923 they were down to an average of $4.15 a day. In addition to restoration of the 1920 wage level, the workers were demanding a reduction of working hours. At that time workers in production departments at the Sydney steel plant worked a twelve-hour shift six days a week with the night shift working a twenty-four-hour shift at the change-over once every two weeks. The workers wanted an eight-hourday. When the union submitted its demands in March, 1923, the company made its rejection public, announcing that it aimed to maintain the open shop; that there would be no check-off of union dues, and no wage increases. The final result was that on June 28, 1923, the union declared a strike. The management of the plant announced the organization of a "defence force" of 400 "faithful employees...armed with iron bars." Armed forces of the state from Toronto and London, Ontario, again invaded Cape Breton Island and the Nova Scotia provincial government added its mounted provincial police. There were 2,000 uniformed soldiers and policemen in the town of Sydney in addition to the company's 400 goons—an armed strike-breaker for every worker on strike.

A veritable reign of terror was launched in Sydney and the adjacent mining towns. The office of the steelworkers' union and the homes of its officers were raided daily. An officer commanding mounted provincials ordered his men to ride into a crowd of 1,000 people in and around a railway underpass on the pretext that it was necessary to "clear the streets." Many were injured, including women and children, some seriously. The office of District 26 U.M.W.A. at Glace Bay Was raided, as were the homes of officers of the miners' union. All these raids were carried out by men in provincial policemen's uniforms, without warrants, with complete disregard for elementary decency, and in several cases with extreme brutality.

The miners of the Glace Bay area, assembled in a huge mass meeting, and by unanimous vote, called upon their executive officers to shut down every mine in the district if the troops and the provincials were not withdrawn. In response to this meeting, the executive officers met with representatives of the provincial government, who would give no commitments about the withdrawal of troops. Another mass meeting was held and a resolution was adopted unanimously, calling upon all miners to leave the pits by midnight of the following day. Every miner in the Glace Bay area obeyed this rank-and-file decision. Following that, the district officers issued a circular to the local unions of the district describing the reasons for the stoppage and calling upon all locals not yet on strike to call meetings immediately, to decide upon action. Every local except one joined in that movement.

Dan Livingstone, the president, and J. B. MacLachlan, the secretary-treasurer of District 26, were arrested. J. B. MacLachlan described his arrest afterward as a kidnapping. Besco, the provincial government, the federal Department of Labor, and the capitalist press carried on a co-ordinated campaign of propaganda to the effect that the steel strike, the miners' sympathy strike and all the violence in Nova Scotia were caused by "foreign agitators." J. B. MacLachlan succeeded in getting bail in spite of the strenuous opposition of the provincial government and he advised the governor-general of Canada that: "If the government will withdraw the troops, the miners will return to the pits immediately." The governor-general declared his intention to "advise" the provincial and federal governments to withdraw their forces but, on that very day, the international executive board of the U.M.W.A. revoked the charter of District 26, removed its elected officers and appointed representatives of the international president to administer the district. The appointed officers ordered the miners back to the pits. On August 1 the Amalgamated Steel Workers Union called off the steelworkers' strike.

Defeat of the strike was followed by brutal prison sentences for "unlawful assembly." Hundreds of the more active union men were blacklisted. The Ukrainian community in Sydney was reduced from several hundreds to a few dozens. Jim MacLachlan was sentenced to two years' imprisonment on the pretence that a letter sent out to the locals of the union had contained seditious libel. The provincial government refused to allow his trial to be held in Glace Bay where the alleged offence was committed–it was held in Halifax.

The real reason for the arrest and imprisonment of Jim MacLachlan was to remove him from the leadership of the miners. He was released from Dorchester Penitentiary in March, 1924, having served only four months of the two years. Miners quit work to greet his return with great spontaneous mass meetings which held up the train. At Glace Bay he was met by a band and thousands of miners who paraded to the theatre where he was welcomed home on behalf of the miners and their families by the mayor, the deposed vice-president of the union, the secretary of the steelworkers union, and by Tom Bell, editor of the *Maritime Labor Herald*. But the international commission remained in control of the union; the miners were stripped of the militant leadership under which they had fought so heroically for more than ten years to establish. the U.M.W.A.

The struggles indicated by the above very sketchy description exerted a very important influence upon the Workers' Party, later the Communist Party, during the 1920's. From the first wage cut imposed by the company in January, 1922, our party was inextricably involved in all the series of great struggles of the miners and steelworkers which continued without interruption until the end of 1925. J. B. MacLachlan and most of the fighting leadership of the miners throughout that period were members of the party. J. B. and Tom Bell were members of the party's Central Committee. All across Canada our party spearheaded the battle for support to the embattled miners and steelworkers, to help feed their children, provide legal defence, to unite the workers around them. On Cape Breton Island the periodic excuses used by the "provincials" for their violent lawlessness was that they were "searching for Reds from Toronto." The party was completely vindicated and rewarded by the fact that, despite all the odds against them the miners and steelworkers halted the offensive of the steel and coal monopoly by their militant struggle.

The defeats suffered by the trade union movement, despite heroic working-class militancy, spotlighted the decisive evil, namely, that the organized workers were but a tiny minority of the working class. As noted earlier, the aggregate membership of all the unions, including the Catholic Syndicates and various independent organizations, was reduced, by the combined effects of the employers' open-shop drive and the policies of the union leaders, to less than a quarter of a million by 1925. Union membership was confined mainly to the "sheltered trades." Except for the workers in the Sydney mill, the basic steel industry was unorganized. Metal fabricating industries, the logging and sawmill industry, automobile, meat-packing, hard-rock mining, textile, aluminum, shipping, asbestos, etc.–the industries in which the great majority of wage earners were employed–were unorganized. Those industries could not be organized on a craft union basis and the bureaucracy of the international unions refused to organize industrial unions. Indeed, they expelled members for even advocating industrial unions. It was evident that the mass industries had to be organized, but it was equally evident that the leaders of the existing trade unions would not do it.

The 1924 national conference of the Trade Union Eductional League pointed to that anomaly and its dire, consequences for the Canadian working class. The conference called upon supporters of the T.U.E.L. everywhere to combine, with the "back-to-the-unions" campaign, movements to "organize the unorganized."[3] The issue was taken up in regional conferences of the T.U.E.L. in Ontario, Alberta and British Columbia, and local industrial conferences were convened to initiate organization.

The loggers were the first to get a functioning organization established, starting in Ontario. Under the leadership of the late Comrade Alf Hautamaki, the Lumberworkers Industrial Union organized camp after camp. At the union's annual convention in 1926 there were thirty-seven delegates, from locals in the Thunder Bay, Algoma, and Hearst areas. The struggles required to build the union were fierce. The lumber bosses stopped at nothing. In October, 1929, two union organizers, Comrades Rosvall and Voutilainen, were murdered in cold blood. But blacklist and violence couldn't stop the union. From modest beginnings made by hard-fighting Finnish lumberjacks, the loggers of northern and northwestern Ontario, built up through twenty-five years of struggle the splendid organization that Hutchison, the president of the International Brotherhood of Carpenters and Joiners, gutted in June, 1951. The Pacific Coast loggers had built a powerful union during and immediately following the First World War. The boss loggers, aided by syndicalist confusion spread by the One Big Union and the I.W.W., destroyed that union. As a result the coast loggers got their organization drive under way somewhat later than in Ontario. They, also from modest beginnings, built a militant fighting union. Later, its president, Harold Pritchett, was elected international president of the International Woodworkers Association when the Canadian and U.S. unions merged.[4]

Organization of the hard-rock miners started with the Porcupine Mineworkers Union (1925), which became part of the Mine Workers Union of the W.U.L. and entered the International Union of Mine, Mill and Smelter Workers in 1936. Organization in the automobile industry was tough. No permanent organization was achieved in the hundred per cent strike at Oshawa in 1927. In the General Motors and Ford plants at Oshawa and Windsor respectively the companies' system of anti-union espionage

46

seemed almost perfect. One after another, union activists were fired and effectively blacklisted from the industry. At last a constituent convention was organized at the Prince George Hotel, Toronto. Delegates representing locals (small and completely underground) in the General Motors and the Ford automobile plants, and some feeder plants in Toronto and St. Catharines, adopted a constitution and a general platform of demands.

The Automobile Workers Industrial Union never achieved bargaining strength however. In 1937 its small underground local in Oshawa succeeded in combining the effects of its propaganda activity with burning resentment against arbitrary company action. Starting with the body department, the entire plant was tied up. The possibility that the A.W.I.U. of Canada might emerge as an open organization could not be allowed to determine what tactics the small local should pursue. Overcoming the reluctance of several of the comrades who had worked so hard and risked so much to maintain their local through the years of underground effort, the decision was made to utilize the strike as a means of organizing all Canadian auto workers in the United Auto Workers of America. After convincing the Oshawa members, J. B. Salsberg, contacted Homer Martin, then president of the U.A.W.A. Martin sent a representative to Oshawa immediately. The strike became a U.A.W. strike and the General Motors plant at Oshawa became a union shop. Unionization of Windsor followed shortly afterwards.

In the steel industry, too, organization was extremely difficult at first. Several local unions were established, but it was years before a number of them were linked together in a functioning union. In steel, also, the obstacle to unionization was the unscrupulous activities of the employers, not lack of interest on the part of the workers. For example, the workers of the National Steel Car plant at Hamilton, Ontario, fought a major strike for six weeks in 1928. That struggle illustrated both the will of the workers to struggle and the fruit of the party's work in developing youthful leadership. Harvey Murphy, then twenty-two years of age, led that strike like a veteran. The union had no treasury, the families of many of the workers went hungry until a relief committee was organized and set to work by a young comrade (Minnie Davis) then twenty years of age.

Textile, furniture, packinghouse workers and others established local unions, fought bitter strikes and learned invaluable lessons. In the Estevan massacre, September 29, 1931, the mounted police shot down peaceful miners as they were assembling for a public strike meeting, killing three and wounding thirteen. Then they hunted down Annie Buller, the miners' guide and inspiration, and sentenced her to two years' imprisonment, literally for the bloody massacre carried out by the R.C.M.P. Troops and tanks patrolled the streets of Stratford, Ontario, in a governmental attempt to intimidate workers. Miners at Flin Flon and Noranda, textile workers in Quebec and Ontario, needle trades workers in Toronto and Montreal, packinghouse workers in Winnipeg, sawmill workers in British Columbia–all defied government and employer violence and organization went on.

As a direct result of the work of our party, the attitude of revolutionary workers to the trade union movement was completely changed before the end of the 1920's. The long-entrenched idea that revolutionary workers should refuse to be members of A.F.L. unions, that they should denounce craft unions as "job trusts" and expend their energies in efforts to build one or the other of the various "perfect-on-paper" revolutionary unions, was completely discredited and rejected by all revolutionary workers. In its place there was established recognition of the fact that the place for militant workers was in the unions which commanded the loyalty and support of the overwhelming majority of the workers. The return of thousands of militants had revitalized the craft-unions in many areas. For the first time in history there were examples of craft unions giving active assistance to the building of industrial unions.

Much of what the party fought for in its battles for

industrial unionism and to organize the unorganized during the 1920's has been achieved now: not always in exactly the way that we then anticipated, but that is not the main consideration. The idea of industrial unionism that the party implanted in the minds and hearts of hundreds of thousands of workers became the vital dynamic driving force of the later campaigns which did establish industrial unions throughout the main industries of Canada. In several industries the unions that were established by the T.U.E.L. or the Workers' Unity League were the organizational beginnings of what are now powerful C.I.O. or A.F.L. unions.

Note

1. *Steps to Power*, pp. 8-10.

2. Pennsylvania, Ohio, Illinois.,

3. The slogan was part of the official program of the T.U.E.L.

4. It is noteworthy that Comrade Pritchett ceased to be international president of the I.W.A. through action of the U.S. government–not by the will of the membership. The U.S. Immigration Department refused to allow him to perform the duties of his office in the United States.

CHAPTER THREE: "The American Way..." in the 1920's

MILITANT LABOR struggles were not the only characteristic of the 1920's. The political climate of that decade was colored by the rise of American imperialism to world primacy. With the tremendous expansion of foreign investment and influence there went also a new cycle of expansion of United States economy, in which Canadian economy shared to some extent. An outgrowth of this new stage of American imperialism was the increasing corruption of trade union leaders. To secure for themselves a share in the "prosperity" of American capitalism, more and more of them used the resources of the unions under their leadership to establish union-financed capitalist enterprises: insurance companies, banks, real-estate companies, even scab industrial concerns.[1]

Along with commitment of the resources of trade unions to capitalist enterprises there went attempts to tie members to the unions through insurance policies and investments, instead of by the struggle for higher wages and better conditions. The unions were made part of the machinery of capitalist management -- in some cases, for example the Amalgamated Clothing Workers, the International Association of Machinists, etc., union leadership sought to replace the capitalist efficiency experts. "Theoretical" and "moral" justification for the brazen betrayals perpetrated by those "misleaders of labor"[2] was attempted by the elaboration of a whole body of propaganda to the effect that, through "Fordism," American capitalism had discovered the secret of permanent prosperity. The "labor" bankers, real-estate speculators, insurance brokers and their paid propagandists declared that all previous experience of the labor movement was now out of date, the teachings of Marx completely discredited, and that the sole but wide-open path forward for the labor movement lay through class collaboration. They described their schemes to transform the unions into capitalist trusts and promoters of speed-up systems as "the higher strategy of labor." The Executive Council of the American Federation of Labor carried its anti-working-class doctrine to such a length as to invite a hundred right-wing social democrats from Germany to attend the El Paso convention in 1926 as guests "to study the secret of the new American economy." Following the convention, the German right-wing union officials were the guests of the Ford Motor Company. They were taken to Detroit, shown through the Ford plants and lectured concerning Ford methods with a great show of cooperation. The real content of the so-called "union-management cooperation" of that period is illustrated by the fact that, right then, while it was entertaining the A.F.L. leaders and their guests, the Ford company was smashing, by the most ruthless use of labor spies, discharge and blacklist, an attempt being made by A.F.L. unions to organize the Ford workers. The visit of the right-wing social democrats put an end to even the pretence of a campaign. Hundreds of workers who had been defying the company's intimidation threw up their hands in disgust. Even the joint organizing committee sponsored by the A.F.L. dissolved.

The political character of the policies developed by the right-wing union leaders and socialists all over the United States and Canada during that period showed their acceptance of the perspective aimed at by the bankers and the manufacturers' associations. They became conscious agents of the capitalist class within the labor movement. Accepting the capitalist perspective, they moved to emasculate the trade union movement and destroy its fighting spirit. When the left wing mobilized the workers for effective opposition, the bureaucrats resorted to a vicious anti-working-class campaign to "clean out the Reds."

The above characterization of the situation in the trade union movement applies in every detail to both Canada and the United States. There was little trade union organization in Canada

51

except the international unions. International officers interfered in the affairs of Canadian locals with even less regard for the will of the Canadian membership than they show today. Charters were lifted by presidents in the United States who disdained to hide their contempt for the small Canadian membership. Workers were expelled from unions for "advocating industrial unionism." Hundreds of workers were excluded from union membership for refusing to incur large obligations for life insurance in the company headed by the president of their union. Because independent working-class political action was contrary to the political philosophy of the capitalist-minded bureaucrats who dominated the A.F.L., Canadian locals of the international unions and trades and labor councils were ordered to disaffiliate from the Canadian Labor Party on pain of expulsion from the "international" trade union movement. Expulsion didn't mean simply that the expelled local or council could henceforth pursue its own course: it meant that another local or council was set up. By collaboration between the top union leadership and the bosses, the new one usually became the only organization through which the workers could secure employment.

During that period a change took place in the attitude of monopoly capital towards the trade union movement. The limited success achieved in their open-shop drive, at enormous expense to their corporations, had shown the more far-sighted of them that the trade union movement could not be destroyed or rendered incapable of militant struggle by the traditional methods of open warfare against the idea of trade unionism. To an increasing extent the "labor relations" experts of monopoly-capital were searching for more efficient methods of blunting the militancy of the workers and beheading their efforts to secure improved wages and conditions.

Collaboration with right-wing union officials was already an established practice. The Dominion Coal Company collaborated with reactionary officers of the Provincial Workmen's Association for years to keep the United Mine

Workers of America out of Nova Scotia, because the movement of the U.M.W.A. was headed by J. B. MacLachlan and supported by the most militant miners. But, during the very year in which the Dominion Coal Company was forced at last to recognize the U.M.W.A. in Nova Scotia (1919), the international officers of the U.M.W.A. were collaborating with the mining companies in Alberta to defeat and destroy a united movement by the miners for more militant unionism in that province. The U.M.W.A (which the mine bosses had fought bitterly up to that time) was granted a district-wide contract, a closed shop and the check-off, thus making every worker in the mines a member of the U.M.W.A. by the will of the Colliery Managers' Association. Whereas in Nova Scotia it was the members of the U.M.W.A. who had been victimized, in Alberta the miners who were organizing a Canadian union were excluded from the mines by the technique of hiring only through the U.M.W.A. office. In that way, well-known militants were excluded from the mines for years. Most of them got back to work only after the Workers' Party and the T.U.E.L. campaign to reunite the trade union movement had succeeded to the extent of getting them back into the U.M.W.A. -- after which its leadership and its policies in District 18 were changed again rapidly.

Such collaboration had not been the general policy of monopoly-capital. When practised it had been in the nature of a temporary acceptance of what big business management considered at the time to be a lesser evil. But, in the second half of the 1920's, organized collaboration with the right-wing officialdom of the trade union movement became the main policy of monopoly-capital towards the trade union movement.

In some cases, typified by numerous experiences of the unions organized by the party and the Workers' Unity League, employers would invite reactionary leadership of other unions to "come in." In such cases, a closed-shop agreement and the check-off were utilized to ensure that' every worker employed paid dues to the collaborating outfit, thus ensuring that only the most class-conscious workers would remain members of the militant union. Such was the evolution of the class-collaboration technique by which reactionary trade union leaderships serve monopoly-capital against the working class today.

During the second half of the 1920's the capitalist class and its governments resorted increasingly to open reaction as an integral part of their conscious turn to fascism and imperialist war. Use of the state machinery against the labor movement became more open. Contemporaneously with the increasing use of R.C.M.P. spies in labor organizations and of police and troops against strikers, there was a marked change in the attitude of local police authorities to working-class activities. The change was too general and uniform to have been accidental. Street meetings, which had been the traditional form of public expression for the working-class movement for decades, were subjected to violent persecution which was developed rapidly to systematic suppression. Local police authorities sought to bar the left-wing movement from the use of public halls. In Toronto, for example, Chief of Police Draper prohibited public speech in any language other than English in licensed halls. A member of the party, Albert Greaves, was arrested and charged -- for speaking French. Operators of licensed halls were warned by the police that any who rented his premises to the Communist Party or an organization which supported the party, without first securing permission from the police, would be liable to lose his licence. At first some operators ignored the warning. In one such case police officers of the so-called "anti-subversive" squad tried to create a panic among 1,300 workers crowded into the Standard Theatre and almost succeeded. They detonated a stink bomb on the stage while Beckie Buhay was speaking. When Philip Halperin, then editor of *Der Kamf*, appealed to the crowd to remain calm and not to play into the hands of the police provocateurs, he was arrested and charged with disturbing the peace.

Organized efforts at suppression of the public activities of the party reached a critical stage in the latter part of the decade.

The struggles that raged all over the country at that time were typified by the "battles of Queen's Park" in Toronto through 1929 and 1930. Those were, in fact, attempts by the workers to maintain their traditional right to hold meetings in Queen's Park -- a right then being challenged for the first time since 1872.

The first violent effort to destroy this traditional right was made by the Toronto police department on August 1, 1929. Some 12,000 Toronto workers were gathered in the park for the annual "No More War" day. At the last moment Chief Constable Draper allowed it to be known that he intended to prevent the meeting. When the speaker and the chairlady approached the bandstand they were seized by half a dozen policemen. The speaker was beaten, several of his teeth being knocked out by a police billy. The chairlady,[3] eighteen years of age, was roughly mauled and insulted. As though this were a signal, scores of mounted policemen rode into the crowd using their whips right and left against everybody who didn't run. Simultaneously, motorcycle police rode into the small knots of workers missed by the cossacks. The meeting was smashed.

There was some considerable public perturbation at what the daily papers described as the "high-handed" methods used by the police department. Assuming that the widely-expressed public disapproval would deter the chief constable from repeating such tactics, the Toronto City Committee of the party called another meeting to carry through the annual anti-war demonstration two weeks later. The police department was not deterred by the public protests, however. The only difference in their tactics was that, the second time, the chief constable did not announce his intention to break up the meeting and the police in the park did not limit their actions to simply driving the workers away. This time, the speaker was given a merciless, protracted public beating, including brutal kicking while two policemen held him. After that, every worker who did not run at full speed was beaten. A university professor attracted to the park by the newspaper protests against the tactics of the police at the first meeting, was knocked down, kicked until he got up again and then beaten because he protested.[4]

Such were the conditions in which the party had to carry on its public activities at the end of the 1920's. As part of their general campaign of persecution, the police succeeded in getting the party evicted from its national office on the pretence that the building was a fire trap. (Promptly after the eviction of the party the building was utilized as a rooming house -- it is still so used.)

* * *

The rapid spread of the Communist movement throughout Canada during the 1920's was accompanied by a certain lowering of its theoretical level. Many workers had been attracted by the practical work and unwavering devotion of the Communists, particularly its battle against secessionism, its campaigns against wage cuts and to organize the unorganized. Other workers were attracted to the movement by the party's unwavering struggle against the class-collaboration policies pursued by the international officialdom and the unscrupulousness of the campaign launched against the Communists by the A.F.L. bureaucracy. But the activities which proved it to be "A Party of Action" had not been accompanied by equally systematic efforts within the party on the front of theoretical work. The party membership had not yet grasped the full import of Lenin's emphasis upon the fact that "without a revolutionary theory there can be no revolutionary movement." While self-criticism was mentioned frequently in quotations or in comments upon discussions taking place in other countries, there was not then a full understanding of the vital significance of criticism and self-criticism as the law of growth of Communist parties. As a result the party was vulnerable to highsounding propaganda even when it was based upon false theories. Some party members were confused by the propaganda about "permanent prosperity" in North America. Others were attracted by the radical-sounding phrase-mongering of the Canadian followers of Leon Trotsky

Because the party's leadership had failed to press the fight for theory, infiltration of bourgeois influences into the party did not always immediately become evident. Often, ideas which were basically revisionist were masked successfully for considerable time. The followers of Trotsky developed to a high degree a technique of screening their opposition to Marxism-Leninisin by emphasis upon matters of detail and methods of application. Later, when a group of leaders of the party and mass organizations adopted the bourgeois theory of "American exceptionalism," they used a similar technique.

The first of these revisionist tendencies to show itself within the party (exposure of which forced the other tendencies into the open) was that represented by the Canadian followers of Leon Trotsky. Adhering closely to the general political standpoint of Trotsky himself, and using the same tactics, his Canadian followers presented their opportunistic petty-bourgeols theories under a screen of "leftist" demagogy.

Trotsky himself had carried on opposition to Lenin's policies for a decade before the Russian Revolution. At the time of the Russian Revolution he acknowledged that Lenin had been correct, but he reverted to opposition again before Lenin died. In a letter to one of his American followers, Shactman, on December 10, 1930, he explained that since 1923 he had been a member of an organized bloc of heterogeneous elements who agreed with each other only in their opposition to the policies of the Communist Party of the Soviet Union (Bolsheviks).

For all the superficial appearance of brilliance in his polemical writings, Trotsky demonstrated an inability to grasp the fundamental dialectics of the revolutionary struggle. In opposition to the great program of socialist construction in the Soviet Union he catered to capitalist hopes -- and illusions -- with assertions that "the law of labor-productivity" would render it impossible for the Soviet people to build up a largescale socialist industry in the face of the inevitable flood of cheap commodities from the West. He failed completely to understand that the law of socialist revolution is higher than the law of labor-productivity. Lacking faith in the working class, he denied that the dictatorship of the proletariat, in alliance with the poor and middle peasantry throughout the vast Soviet Union, could build a new socialist economic system. On the basis of a completely erroneous conception of the operation of economic laws he, in alliance with Bukharin and the "right opposition" in the Soviet Union, opposed the Lenin-Stalin policy of building a large-scale unified socialist economy. He proposed instead that the peasants should revert to simple commodity production. In that he contradicted what Lenin had defined as "the elementary propositions of Marxism concerning the inevitability of capitalist development where commodity production exists." Lenin continued, "Marxism teaches that a society which is based on commodity production and which has commercial intercourse with civilized capitalist nations, itself invariably takes the road of capitalism at a certain stage of its development."[5] On the other hand, Trotsky insisted, ridiculously, in the 1920's that only the dictatorship of the proletariat could solve the democratic tasks which were then on the order of the day for the Chinese Revolution.

Stalin's uncompromising battle against the opposition of the Trotskyites and the right liquidators in the Soviet Union was, in fact, a battle against plans and proposals to establish conditions which would have facilitated the growth of capitalism in the Soviet Union. Stalin's battle was based firmly and simply upon the line of struggle embodied in Lenin's life's work; keyed to maintenance and continued strengthening of the alliance between the proletariat and the poor peasantry, neutralizing the middle peasantry and eliminating every vestige of capitalism and capitalist-class influence.

Trotsky's role confirmed in every respect the characterization of him written by Lenin in 1914. "Trotsky has never yet held a firm opinion on any important question of Marxism. He always manages to 'creep into the chinks' of this or that difference of opinion and desert one side for the other."[6]

Unable to win popular support on the basis of their policies, Trotsky and his allied oppositionists tried to discredit the plans for socialist construction by fomenting kulak opposition to collectivization, the murder of party leaders, e.g., Sergei Kirov, destructive sabotage and planned disorganization. Frustrated by the revolutionary vigilance of the workers, they turned to the path of counter-revolution and entered the service of the imperialists. Offering in advance to agree to Japanese seizure of the eastern maritime provinces, German seizure of the Ukraine and Anglo-French domination of the Caucasus, in payment for imperialist military assistance to them in overthrowing Soviet power, they served the imperialists immediately as spies and provocateurs. In the course of his trial Bukharin described how they received 250,000 gold marks per year from the German government in payment for military and economic intelligence work and organization of sabotage within the Soviet Union. When a leading U.S. Trotskyite was sent to Norway in 1936 for personal consultation with Trotsky concerning some questions about which there were sharp differences within the Trotskyite sect in the United States, he returned to report that "the Master" had shown very little interest in their differences but had insisted that the Trotskyites in North America should show more interest in his plans "to organize a counter-revolution against the Soviet Union." As Stalin pointed out in 1937, Trotskyism ceased to be a political trend in the working class. "It has changed from the political trend in the working class which it was seven or eight years ago, into a frantic and unprincipled gang of wreckers, diversionists, spies and murderers acting on the instruction of the intelligence services of foreign states."[7]

The difference between the Canadian followers of Trotsky and the other oppositionists was that the Trotskyites concentrated their attention upon opposition to the policies being pursued in the Soviet Union, with noisy, radical-sounding arguments to the effect that "it is impossible to build socialism in one country." They aped Trotsky in his transition to open counter-revolution with assertions that there is no socialism in the Soviet Union, therefore the Soviet government must be overthrown.

The right liquidators in the Soviet Union also had their organized followers in North America. The right opposition eventually set up an open party organization in the United States and Canada under the leadership of Lovestone, the ex-general-secretary of the Communist Party of the United States. It sought an understanding with American imperialism. Lovestone and his followers tried to justify their renegacy by the pretence that the class-collaboration policies being pursued by the A.F.L. bureaucracy and the right-wing Socialists mirrored a fundamental difference between North American capitalism and capitalism as Marx had known it. This came to be known as the theory of "North American exceptionalism." Its essential argument was that North American capitalism in its imperialist stage was so powerful that by subordinating other capitalist countries, exploiting them as well as colonial countries in its own interests, it could prevent economic crisis in the United States. American economy was therefore, according to Lovestone, "exceptional" in that it was immune from the economic laws of motion of capitalism and, therefore, from the periodic crises which Marx had shown to be an inseparable feature of the economic laws of motion of capitalism.

Lovestone's supporters in Canada were not all motivated solely by belief in the theory of "American exceptionalism." In the conditions of sharpening police persecution and efforts at suppression with the increasing difficulties of extending the party's public work, some members of the Communist Party, including some members of its leadership, became receptive to the idea of class collaboration. Starting with resistance to the mobilization of mass public working-class action against police terror, such people soon sought to justify their passivity by the arguments of "American exceptiorialism." It was a time in Canada when, as Lenin had pointed out in the Russia of 1902, "the fashionable preaching of opportunism went hand in hand with an infatuation for the narrowest forms of practical activity."[8]

In Canada, as in other countries, what appeared on the surface as two rival oppositions were in reality but the two wings of one political opposition, as was demonstrated when they eventually merged their organizations.

At first, however, they appeared to be in opposition to each other as well as to the party. Maurice Spector, then editor of *The Worker*, reported on the Sixth World Congress of the Communist International to a public meeting in Toronto in October, 1928. The content of his report was such that, following the meeting, a number of party members headed by Beckie Buhay demanded of the chairman that the matter be dealt with by the Political Committee of the party. The following day, to the surprise of the other members of the Political Committee, Jack MacDonald, the general secretary of the party, anticipated discussion of the question by moving that an emergency meeting of the Central Committee of the party be convened immediately to investigate the "political position of Comrade Spector." When the emergency meeting of the Central Committee convened, MacDonald sprang another surprise by producing copies of corespondence between Spector and the leaders of the Trotskyite organization in the United States, elaborating plans to split the Communist Party and establish a Trotskyite organization in Canada. Exposed, and refusing to repudiate the activities that he had carried on secretly until then, Spector was suspended by the Central Committee. In cooperation with heterogeneous elements and the police, he called a public meeting at the Standard Theatre and tried with very limited success to launch a Trotskyite party.

MacDonald met the dissatisfaction of the majority of the members of the Central Committee at his failure to report possession of the evidence against Spector earlier by "explaining" that the secretary of the American party, Lovestone, had only recently come into possession of the evidence by a peculiar accident and had supplied it to MacDonald because of their close personal cooperation. MacDonald proceeded immediately on a national tour to report on the matter' and alert the membership against Spector's Trotskyite activities. He had got no farther than the Head of the Lakes when reports came back to Toronto that the political line he was advocating against Spector was not the line of the world Communist movement but Lovestone's line of "American exceptionalism." In Winnipeg, Tom McEwen, district organizer of the party, was compelled to take public exception to elements of MacDonald's report. MacDonald did not complete his tour. He returned suddenly to Toronto where several members of the national leadership confronted him with the question as to his fundamental political position. That issue dominated all party discussions, the life of the party in fact, from then until the Sixth National Convention held in May, 1929.

In the public debates that were held, as well as in executive discussions, the Lovestonites, of whom MacDonald was the leader and main spokesman, tried to win support for the theory that Canadian economy, by virtue of its close ties with United States economy, was immune to the danger of capitalist crisis and, therefore, it was wrong to base the line of the party upon the prospect of economic crisis and increasing radicalization of the masses. A minority of the members of the party leadership opposed that point of view. They based themselves upon the economic laws of motion of capitalism as revealed by Marx and the thesis adopted by the Sixth World Congress of the Communist International. To the concrete question posed in numerous public meetings -- "Can the perspective of Canadian economy be determined on the basis of the economic laws of motion of capitalism revealed by Marx? -- MacDonald and his Lovestonite supporters answered No!; the minority answered Yes!

Conflict over that question dominated the Sixth National Convention of the party. When Secretary MacDonald called his supporters into a caucus to prepare their slate for the election of the new Central Cominittee, it was revealed that, despite the evident influence of the minority in the debates, 65 of the 78 accredited delegates were MacDonald supporters. The result was that the Lovestonites elected the Central Committee of their choice. Considering it tactically wise, they elected three members of the minority also: namely, Buck, Smith and Bruce. When the convention adjourned, it appeared that the Lovestonites had won the party.

Life, however -- which in our case means mainly the working class -- decided otherwise. The Lovestoneites had the votes in the national convention but the position of the minority had corresponded with the basic economic and political realities. Despite the frantic efforts of the capitalist press and the stockateers to maintain the illusion that Canadian economy was thriving, signs that its contradictions were acute were becoming evident. Side by side with reports of new high peaks of profits, unemployment was increasing also. Over-expansion of industry revealed itself. Some new plants never operated at capacity. The comrades who had fought Trotskyism and opposed the policies based upon the theory of "American exceptionalism" continued their battle after the national convention. Leading officers of some of the mass organizations supported the Lovestoneite position of MacDonald but the minority was winning ever wider support among the most active members of the party as a whole, including the activists of the organizations, the leaders of which were supporting the Lovestone position. The position of the minority was supported by the whole leadership of the Young Communist League. The membership of the party was recognizing that the minority was fighting for a correct Communist position. With that recognition support for the minority was growing rapidly. As a result MacDonald found his position so contradictory that, six weeks after the convention, he called a special meeting of the new Central Committee (July 12, 1929). Right at the opening of the meeting, he informed the Central Committee that, due to the conflict within the party, his position was untenable and lie had therefore decided to resign. In the same statement, he nominated for the office of general secretary Tim Buck, who had opposed Trotskyite tendencies within the Central Committee since Spector had first revealed them in 1925, and who had been the main spokesman for the minority through the pre-convention discussion and the convention debates. All except three of the members of the Central Committee were ardent supporters of MacDonald yet, after some perfunctory debate, his resignation was accepted and Comrade Buck elected general secretary. The following day, a carefully prepared statement over the name of MacDonald and naming several members of the Central Committee as being aligned with him, appeared in papers edited by his supporters, calling upon the workers to abandon the Communist Part of Canada and establish a new organization.

It was evident that MacDonald's resignation and the election of a new secretary had been carefully staged in the belief that it would help to isolate the minority and tend to encourage members to follow MacDonald out of the party. As we shall see later, he underestimated both the intelligence and the loyalty of the majority of the party membership. Within a relatively short time, the organization that he established and the organization established earlier by Spector were compelled to join forces in an attempt to maintain an appearance of strength. Within a few years it disappeared completely as an organized political force.

Note

1. Such as, for example, Coal River Collieries, a scab mine owned and operated by one of the capitalist offshoots of the Brotherhood of Locomotive Engineers.

2. W. Z. Foster's description of them.

3. *Lillian Himmelfarb.*

4. Professor Meek of the University of Toronto.

5. "The Right of Nations to Self-Determination." *Selected Works.* Vol. 4, p. 286.

6. V. I. Lenin, "Two Tactics of Social Democracy in the Democratic Revolution." Chapter 6, *Selected Works.* Vol. 3, p. 74,

7. *Mastering Bolshevism.*

8. "What Is To Be Done?" *Selected Works.* Vol. 2, p. 47.

CHAPTER FOUR: The End of "Permanent Prosperity"

THREE MONTHS after MacDonald launched his party to propagate the theory of "American exceptionalism," his vaunted, "permanent prosperity" came to a sudden and cataclysmic end. Stock markets crashed -- first in New York, then around the capitalist world. Factories closed by the hundreds, the prices of raw materials collapsed Farmers, small-business and professional people, passed swiftly from illusions of affluence to utter despair. Overshadowing all the tragedies of the middle classes was the utter catastrophe that the crisis brought upon the working class.

The fact that the Workers' Unity League was founded three weeks after the great Wall Street crash was partly coincidence, but it illustrated the correspondence between the attitude of the party's new leadership and the trend of development. The W.U.L. was established to meet a need that had been developing for some considerable time -- the need for co-ordinating the efforts to build industrial unions in the "open-shop" industries, to develop the struggle for national unemployment insurance, to extend the campaign for independent working-class political action, for national and international trade union unity. By the time the national conference which founded the W.U.L. was held another need had become urgent: namely, the need to win immediate relief for the hundreds of thousands of families whose bread-winners were suddenly and hopelessly unemployed.

The program of the W.U.L. was as follows:
1. Organize the Unorganized Workers.
2. National Non-Contributory Unemployment Insurance. Work or Full Maintenance.
3. Unity of the Employed and Unemployed.

4. An Emergency Program of Home Construction.
5. Industrial Unionism.
6. Independent Working-Class Political Action.
7. Nationalization of Key Industries.
8. Trade Union Unity in One National Centre.
9. World Trade Union Unity.
10. Canadian Trade with the Soviet Union.

Immediately after its establishment the Workers' Unity League launched a great national campaign to organize the masses of unemployed workers and to unite the labor movement in support of its draft parliamentary bill for national unemployment insurance. Along with the battle for the elementary needs of the unemployed, campaigns to organize the unorganized workers were developed in a score of industries.

Federal general elections were held in August, 1930. The Liberals and Tories had a complete electoral monopoly. The Communist Party of Canada was the only other national party. The election campaigns of its candidates were beset by so much police persecution, open gang violence organized by the old party candidates and complete boycott by the capitalist press that the majority of Canadians were given the impression that our party was in some way or other illegal. The Liberals under Mackenzie King contented themselves with a routine, uninspired, defeatist campaign. Their leadership didn't want to win. The Tories, under their new leader, the militant reactionary, multi-millionaire R. B. Bennett, waged an aggressive and unscrupulous winning campaign. Bennett promised each section of the country what the majority of the voters there felt they needed most. To the workers of Central Canada he promised jobs; to the manufacturing and commercial interests, more trade with the Empire and increased protection of the home market. To the interests depending upon the export of natural products, particularly the farmers, he promised to "blast our way into the markets of the world."

The election marked a conscious turn of Canadian capitalists towards policies of increasingly open reaction, fascism and war. The Tory victory was a part of the turn being made by world imperialism at that time. The, extent to which R. B. Bennett actually believed the things he said is beyond the scope of this work. It is evident that he suffered from illusions concerning the vitality of capitalism and the possibility of solving its deepening inherent contradictions by traditional capitalist techniques. He believed uncritically in the eternity of the profit system. The real difference between him and the Liberals was that he apparently really believed in liberal economics, with the qualification that he did not conceal his opinion that the function of capitalist government was to serve monopoly capital.

His first act when fie became prime minister was to convene a special session of parliament. Its announced purpose was to deal with the emergency created by the crisis. His method of meeting the crisis was to increase the tariff against textiles and other consumer goods imported into Canada. He increased the cost of living for Canadian people despite falling world prices. That and other similar public actions were accompanied by the adoption of secret orders-in-council to protect the banks and insurance companies from the consequences of their attempts to make speculative profits out of the recent inflationary boom. The "emergency session" did not propose one measure to help the millions of workers, farmers, professional and smallbusiness people who were suffering actual want as a result of the crisis. Later his government dipped heavily into the public treasury to provide very large financial assistance to the Canadian Pacific Railway with which he had been intimately associated for many years.

There was no unemployment insurance in Canada at that time. The Communist Party alone had carried on a consistent all-sided struggle for national unemployment insurance. In spite of the repeated warnings uttered by the Communist Party that signs of an impending crisis were multiplying, and its demands upon the federal government for measures to protect the workers and farmers against its effects, no action had been taken. The Liberal government under Mackenzie King had evaded responsibility on the plea that it lacked constitutional authority. The Tory government under Bennett, which followed, concentrated its attention and energy upon enacting measures to protect the interests of big business at the expense of the working class. The municipalities, upon whom the immediate responsibility fell, were completely unable to cope with the problem created by needs of such magnitude.

Hundreds of farmers were being evicted from their farms. Working-class home-owners were losing their homes (in Toronto and the Yorks alone 12,000 eviction notices were issued during the year 1931). Small business men were losing their businesses. Tens of thousands of young men wandered back and forth across the country in a futile search for jobs or food. Their plight evoked the term "the lost generation."

Eventually the Bennett government did take action to deal with the problem represented by the tens of thousands of unemployed young men. It established "labor camps," operated by the Department of National Defence. Single men who applied for public relief were herded into those camps across the country and put to work building roads, clearing the bush, etc., at the wage of twenty cents per day. They became known as "Bennett's slave camps."

All the illusions about "permanent prosperity" were dissolved by the facts of life. The Trotskyites and the "American exceptionalists" merged their organizations and tried to secure support by attacking the Communist Party "from the 'left'." But the only coherent program of national action to meet the effects of the crisis was the one put forward by the Communist Party of Canada. It included carefully worked out proposals for federal, provincial and municipal cooperation in the launching of projects to provide jobs at trade union rates for 200,000 workers throughout the country. It proposed large-scale slum clearance and home building. It proposed reforestation of the eastern slopes of the Rockies, conservation of their waters and harnessing the

Saskatchewan River to develop hydro-electric power and irrigate hundreds of thousands of acres of Prairie farms. It proposed undertakings in every part of Canada for the improvement and enrichment of the country. It proposed feed and seed loans and moratoria to protect farmers from loss of their farms. It proposed moratoria to protect small home-owners and immediate relief for every Canadian family in need. The program envisaged an expenditure by the federal government of $400,000,000 through 1931 and 1932.

The party and the Workers' Unity League, supported by hundreds of local unions, farmers and other democratic organizations, developed a nation-wide campaign around this program. The Workers' Unity League, through the left-wing unions, mobilized the workers who were employed to support their unemployed fellow-workers who were being united for self-defence in the local councils of the National Unemployed Workers' Association. The W.U.L.'s inspired campaign and its defiance of Bennett's "Iron Heel" threat stirred the working people. It was the final factor which caused Sam Scarlett to renounce his lifelong advocacy of syndicalism. Sam joined our party in the midst of severe repression. He was a tower of strength in our movement for the rest of his life. During the same period, militant Prairie farmers, under the leadership of Walter Wiggins, J. M. Clarke, L. P. MacNamee and other members of the party, united their forces in the Farmers' Unity League. In addition to their desperate need for feed for their stock, food for their families, seed for sowing, they were rendered desperate by mass evictions and sheriffs' sales which then characterized the Prairie provinces.

To its slogan for the unemployed workers: "Work or Full Maintenance," the party added its call to the farmers: "Don't be Starved Out, Don't be Frozen Out, Don't be Sold Out -- Fight!" Along with the unemployed workers the farmers followed the party's advice. Vigilance committees were established in scores of townships. Sheriffs' sales were transformed into comedies by

70

organized bidding on the part of the farmers in which no neighbor would bid against another, and the entire stock, furniture and equipment of a farm would be purchased by the neighbors for a total of twenty dollars or so, after which it would be given back to its original owner and the sheriff would be warned off the property.

The national campaign for the emergency program to meet the farm and unemployment crisis culminated in a delegation representing conferences held in every large industrial centre from coast to coast and four regional farm conferences. The delegation, headed by Tom McEwen, the general secretary of the Workers' Unity League, proceeded to Ottawa where it met R. B. Bennett and most of the members of his cabinet in July, 1931. The government rejected all the proposals of the delegation on the pretence that it was merely a group of "foreign agents." The prime minister personally threatened Tom McEwen with deportation.

Within less than a month of meetingt hat delegation, R. B. Bennett, in cooperation with the Tory provincial government of Ontario, resorted to the use of Section 98 against the Communist Party of Canada.

CHAPTER FIVE: The Test of a Party

THE TEST OF A PARTY, as Lenin pointed out, is its attitude towards its own mistakes. During and immediately after its election the new leadership of the party fell considerably short of a Leninist attitude in that respect. Faced with the task of overcoming the theoretical weaknesses which had facilitated the Trotskyite and Lovestoneite attacks upon party unity, the new leadership concentrated an energetic ideological campaign against those two anti-Leninist tendencies, but failed to recognize the very serious weaknesses in its own theoretical work.

The new leadership was in error on the question of the status of Canada and, therefore, of the perspectives of Canadian development. The importance of this question may be illustrated by the changes that had taken place since we had first issued the slogan of "Canadian Independence." By 1929 the Canadian bourgeoisie was exercising sovereign authority in all distinctly Canadian affairs. With the merging of bank and industrial capital, the rise to power of the finance-capitalist oligarchy and the increasing participation of the Canadian monopolists in the imperialist struggle for division and re-division of the world market, Canada had become an imperialist state. The monopolists maintained vestigial forms of colonial relationships to Britain as barriers between their monopolistic privileges and the advancing forces of the workers and farmers. But, while preserving these obsolete forms of colonial subordination, the Canadian monopolists were already looking towards a junior partnership in United States imperialism for themselves. The change in the status and the aims of the capitalist class had not brought national sovereignty to the people of our country. On the contrary, as events have shown, the Canadian monopolists deliberately betrayed the century-old dream of Canadian independence for their personal profit and class privileges. At the same time, however, the change had rendered the slogans of the struggle for Canadian independence from Britain obsolete.

Instead of recognizing the character of the change that had taken place, the new party leadership put its demand for independence from Britain at the centre of all its political work. It dressed up the demand for "Canadian independence" in an elaborate, almost fantastic argument that independence from Britain was essential to avoid the danger of Canada becoming the battleground in a threatening Anglo-American imperialist war. The effect of this false theory was to make the Communist Party an ideological ally of bourgeois nationalism which developments had already made reactionary. The new path of the proletarian struggle in Canada was determined by the domination of monopoly-capitalism and the anti-national imperialist aims of the finance-capitalist oligarchy. Events had rendered obsolete the idea of national struggle for freedom from British imperialism. The main enemy of the Canadian workers was now Canadian imperialism. The most dire immediate threats against the Canadian people now came from the Canadian monopolists and their anti-Canadian aims. The immediate and pressing need of the party was to concentrate every ounce of its energy to prepare the workers for sharp struggles which loomed ahead.

Thus, the leadership which had fought against the Trotskyite and right liquidationist revisionism was itself leading the party along a false path. Federalistic tendencies bad been developed systematically by MacDonald and his supporters and attempts to combat them were weakened by the errors of the new leadership.

Again it was the youthful members of the party who challenged the incorrect theories. Headed this time by Leslie Morris, Sam Carr, John Weir and Oscar Ryan, they challenged the "Canadian Independence" slogan and called for re-examination of Canada's political perspective. The reply of the party's political bureau was a lengthy and involved attempt to prove the validity of the "Canadian Independence" slogan. The attitude of the membership to that defence is illustrated by the fact that it became known simply as "the 24-page document." However, by dint of earnest, widespread and protracted discussion and a sincere desire to achieve a correct Marxist policy, the leadership did belatedly recognize the change that had taken place in the status of Canada. In the spring of 1930 the Political Bureau repudiated the estimation of Canada as a colony and withdrew its "Canadian Independence" slogan. Incidentally, it should be added that the resolution announcing that repudiation was simultaneously the first official document of our party which specifically described the new character of the Canadian state: an imperialist state, in which the fundamenal line of class conflict is between the interests of the working class allied with the democratic farmers and urban middle-class people, and the anti-social predatory imperialist ambitions of monopoly-capital.

Realization that persistence in our error had undermined efforts to improve the theoretical work of our party, combined with the repeated emphasis by Stalin during that period on the fundamental importance of criticism and self-criticism within parties, resulted in the opening up of a party discussion for the clarification of the party's estimation of Canadian perspectives and preparation for a national convention. For reasons over which the party had no control the convention wasn't held. Police repression had become increasingly violent after the election of the Tory Bennett government in August, 1930. By the technique of breaking up meetings, arresting literature distributors, raiding party offices on the flimsiest of pretexts, etc., similar in all respects to the methods by which the Duplessis government uses its Padlock Law in Quebec today, the governments, federal and provincial, had imposed conditions of semi-legality upon our party. Eventually we were compelled to, limit the national gathering to an extended conference of the Central Committee with leading members engaged in mass public activities in each province.

The plenum met in February, 1931, in Hamilton. It was

raided on the very first day. None of the delegates was arrested; indeed, the policemen were very unsure of themselves because of the evident illegality of their action, but it was impossible to continue in that hall. The plenum was moved to another building in Hamilton only to be asked by the caretaker not to come back the second day because he "had received a warning from the police." At that, the presidium of the plenum decided that if it was to be held at all, it must be held underground -- so measures were taken accordingly. Thus the 1931 plenum, which extended over four days and marked a very important stage in the political development of the party, was held in conditions of complete illegality.

The plenum was self-critical in the extreme. It recorded its decision that the central mistake of the party leadership "consists in the failure to recognize the imperialist interests of the Canadian bourgeoisie and this has led to the false assumption of a basic difference in regard to the path of the proletarian revolution in Canada as compared with other imperialist countries."[1] The plenum called upon the party membership to engage in responsible criticism and self-criticism for the improvement of the party and its work. Its detailed resolution on trade union and economic struggles focussed the energy of the party membership upon the task of organizing the unorganized workers and fighting for progressive policies in the unions that were under reactionary leadership. It adopted a comprehensive program of immediate reforms, it called upon the membership of the party to join in the work of organizing the National Unemployed Workers' Association. It formulated the first fully critical and comprehensive resolution adopted by our party up to that time on its relationship to and program of action for workers in agriculture and working farmers. Similarly it adopted critical resolutions on the responsibility of the party to the youth of Canada and the Young Communist League, to working women and to working-class mass organizations. The latter resolution marked a vital and fruitful turn in the relation of the party to the mass organizations.

The plenum finalized the expulsion of MacDonald and other leading Lovestoneites from the party.

The plenum emphasized the serious shortcomings in the work of the party in French Canada. It emphasized correctly the glaring economic inequalities suffered by the workers in Quebec: "... 4,079 inexperienced women workers in the clothing industry in the district of Montreal receive less than $12 a week ... the wages of inexperienced tobacco workers in the Province of Quebec average $6.94 per week.... In Quebec where the greatest number of women are in industry, infant mortality is higher than in any other province."

The Young Communist League in French Canada had initiated splendid campaigns for the protection of the youth and the organization of young workers. Strikes such as those of the textile workers at Cowansville and elsewhere, led by the Y.C.L., marked the beginning of the emergence of the textile workers of Quebec from industrial peonage. But the party did not yet draw the Leninist conclusion from the fact that the people of French Canada are a nation in every sense of the word and demand for them the full right of national self-determination.

That self-critical national conference of the party adjourned with unanimous adoption of a declaration that, while the fight for unity on the basis of Marxism-Leninism had yet to be completed, the sharpening capitalist crisis and the incontestable spirit of struggle permeating the working class was the guarantee that through single-minded devotion to the cause of the working class and frank self-criticism of its own work, the Communist Party of Canada would make of itself a mass Bolshevik party.

Note

1. Resolutions of the Enlarged Plenum of the Communist Party of Canada, February, 1931, p. 21.

CHAPTER SIX: Suppression and Legality Regained

IN EVERY class society the state is the machinery of the ruling class for the suppression of the exploited class. Throughout the history of organized society until now, each state has been of the character and the form best suited to the maintenance of the power of the ruling class in the prevailing social relations and conditions of production. The means by which the capitalist class maintains its rule and subordinates all the decisive activities of the nation to its interests is, in the final analysis, by use of the machinery of the state, i.e., its state power.

As Lenin emphasized when comparing the proletarian democracy of the Soviet Republics with the bourgeois democracy of the capitalist states: "The most democratic bourgeois republic was never, nor could it be anything else than a machine with which capital suppressed the toilers, an instrument of the political rule of capital, of the dictatorship of the bourgeoisie. The democratic bourgeois republic promised the rule of the majority, it proclaimed the rule of the majority, but it could never put this into effect as long as the private ownership of the land and other means of production existed... In the bourgeois-democratic republic 'freedom' was really freedom for the rich."[1]

In Canada in 1931 the capitalist class headed by Mr. R. B. (Iron Heel) Bennett demonstrated the correctness of Lenin's statement. They sought to buttress their shaken system by the open use of the state machinery against the very forms of democratic action that the capitalist class itself had fought for -- for itself -- less than a century before.

To the sharpening demands and rising temper of the masses of unemployed workers, ruined small businessmen, farmers and dispossessed families, Canadian capitalists, through their federal government, replied with widespread arrests, brazen use of courts as instruments of Tory policy, deportation of scores of militant workers and outlawry of the Communist Party of Canada.

On August 11, 1931, the R.C.M.P. carried out simultaneous raids upon party offices and the homes of party leaders in various parts of the country. The home of each member of the Political Bureau of the party and of other leading comrades, for example, John Boychuk, Toronto, were raided. In addition, the R.C.M.P. seized members of the Political Bureau wherever they happened to be at seven o'clock Eastern Standard Time that evening. Tom Hill was in a restaurant in Cochrane, Ontario. Malcolm Bruce was in Calgary; Sam Carr was in Vancouver. Revealing how close their undercover work had been, the Mounties went straight to the spot where each member of the Political Bureau was at the hour set for the arrests. The one case in which they did not "get their man" emphasized the fact that their undercover work was no emergency surveillance of individuals. Tom McEwen, the comrade they missed, was called away a few minutes before seven -- just before the Mounties swooped down upon his home. The raids on homes were by local, provincial and mounted police. They established a new low level for attempts at police intimidation. Doors were broken open, clothing, bed linen, table linen, books, even the contents of kitchen cabinets, were strewn indiscriminately about the floors. Pictures were torn from their frames. They seized the libraries that working men had spent their lives collecting. Not one of those books was ever restored to its rightful owner. There being nobody home at Tim Buck's house, they unceremoniously pried the front door open, ripping the lock off. They left it that way. The door swung idly until Tim Buck was released on bail.

That wanton destruction was described afterward as a "thorough search for evidence." The statements of governmental spokesmen, such as the attorney-general of Ontario, suggested rather that it was part of a deliberate plan aimed at a wholesale intimidation of workers. It is noteworthy that not one piece of the varied assortment of materials submitted as state evidence in the trial that followed was secured in those raids on homes. Every one of the more than a hundred documents, pamphlets, newspapers, etc., supplied to the prosecutor by the R.C.M.P. was either taken from the offices, taken from the mails, or purchased.

In addition to members of the Political Bureau of the party, two other comrades were arrested. Michael Gilmore was mistaken for Tom McEwen when he went to the latter's home. Tom Cacic was arrested, apparently on general principles, because he went to the national office of the W.U.L. just as the raid got under way. All were committed for trial. Bail for eight of them was set at $20,000 each. For Mike Gilmore, a 17-year-old boy, bail was set at only $10,000 as a sign of the unflinching democracy of Canadian courts. When the crown attorney and Magistrate Brown of Toronto discovered that even the enormity of the bail was not daunting the Canadian Labor Defence League, they resorted to unscrupulous efforts to intimidate workers who offered bail. Each prospective bondsman was subjected to cross-examination in court from the assistant crown attorney. Each one who admitted that he did not personally know the accused on whose behalf he offered bail was promptly disqualified by the magistrate. Those who did declare personal acquaintance were subjected to disgusting and contemptible attempts to intimidate them into withdrawing their offer of bail. Despite all the efforts of the court, however, the $170,000 was posted and all nine were freed on bail until November 2, when the trial started in the Supreme Court of Ontario.

At the opening of the trial Michael Gilmore had to be released when it was proven incontrovertibly that he was not a member of the Communist Party of Canada but only of the Young Communist League. In drafting the indictment, the Crown had failed to mention the Y.C.L. and the judge was unable to find an excuse for making him stand trial.

The trial, the first of its kind in Canada,[2] was a class

trial in every respect. Its purpose was described in the opening words of the special crown prosecutor[3] to the jury. Calling the jurymen's attention to the special character of the trial, and of the law under which it was conducted, he exhorted each member of the jury to keep in mind throughout the trial what he described as the fundamental and first responsibility of the state, "*to protect itself*." To any unprejudiced person who watched that trial it was evident that the prosecutor's exhortation was being obeyed even more by the presiding judge, Mr. Justice Wright, than by the members of the jury. The chief witness for the prosecution was a police spy who had been exposed to the party by a fellow-spy and publicly expelled three and a half years earlier. In an effort to build up a "cloak and dagger" atmosphere, the propaganda department of the R.C.M.P. created a whole body of myths concerning that spy and his supposed activities in the Communist Party, including the completely baseless story that he had held office in leading party committees. That propaganda was a complete fake. Leopold (alias Esselwein) had become a labor spy against his fellow-immigrants from Austria-Hungary in the menial role of reporting to the R.C.M.P. on topics of conversation among his fellow-workers. He "advanced" to the position of a regular, full-time operative within the labor movement when the R.C.M.P. expanded that odoriferous branch of its service at the end of the First World War. He gained recognition within the labor movement in Regina by good work as the secretary of "The Committee for-Medical Aid to Soviet Russia" and as the tireless secretary of the One Big Union in that city. He quit the O.B.U. when the Workers' Party was founded and played an active part in organizing the party's Regina branch, of which he became secretary. He was a member of the International Brotherhood of Painters, Decorators and Paperhangers and a delegate from his local to the Regina Trades and Labor Council. But the R.C.M.P. propaganda that he held high office in the Communist Party was pure invention. The R.C.M.P. transferred him to Toronto in the fall of 1927. From the day of his arrival in Toronto until the public announcement of his expulsion from the party, in May,

1928, he held no office whatsoever, not even in a local party unit; he was a member of the party only.

At the trial, his evidence consisted of word-of-mouth repetition of facts which were already in evidence in the court, in pamphlets and reports, copies of correspondence and newspaper articles. Esselwein did not add one word of evidence to the Crown's case. It was clear that he was produced in brand new Mountie regalia (in which he was extremely uncomfortable) as a stage "prop."

The Crown introduced a mass of documentary evidence, ranging from unsigned carbon copies of alleged personal correspondence to the constitution of the Communist Party of Canada, the *Communist Manifesto* of 1848 and the program of the Communist International. Among the exhibits submitted by the Crown as evidence was a copy of a speech made by Comrade Otto Kuusinen in an international conference on the fight against unemployment. But when the defence tried to introduce the emergency program against unemployment issued by the Communist Party of Canada, it was barred by the judge as "not germane." Similarly, a copy of a letter from Moscow criticizing the party's Draft Agrarian Program was introduced by the Crown without admitting that the letter was written by a Canadian, a member of the Canadian party. But when the defence tried to introduce the Draft Agrarian Program itself, it was also ruled out, with a peevish judicial repetition of "It's the means that we are trying, not all these matters that you are injecting." The prosecution went to great lengths to introduce documents purporting to reveal the history and aims of the party, but the defence was not permitted to deal with the role of the party in the great struggles of the working people and the farmers, either with respect to the fight for reunification of the trade union movement and organization of the unorganized in the early 1920's or the fight against wage cuts, unemployment, evictions and bankruptcy which characterized the situation at the time of the trial.

The class character of the trial was expressed most clearly

by the manner in which the judge rev ealed his prejudice in connection with the fact that one of the accused, Tim Buck, conducted his own defence. The judge demonstratively showed his resentment. He refused to permit Tim Buck to sit at the counsel table. He refused to allow him facilities to take notes of evidence or to have reference material at hand. He compelled him to conform to all the demeaning rules imposed upon the prisoner at the bar, while refusing to grant him the most elementary facilities to practise what is supposed to be the inalienable right of any person charged in a Canadian court of law. As the last defence witness stepped down from the witness box, the judge offered Comrade Buck a perfunctory invitation to address the jury if he so desired. Pointing out that it was within a few minutes of the time for adjournment of the court, Tim Buck asked if he could commence his address to the jury at the opening of court the following morning. The judge replied brusquely that he had "no intention of delaying this case any further." He ruled that if the accused, Buck, wished to address the jury, he must do so then, in which case the court would remain in session until he concluded. He then adjourned the court for five minutes "to give Mr. Buck an opportunity to prepare his address."

The judge was determined that nothing should get into the record concerning the struggles of the working people. He heckled Buck from the opening of the latter's address to the end. He stopped Buck in the midst of his very first sentence, forbidding him to comment upon the fact that governmental publications had reported the activities of the party regularly throughout the ten years just past. When Buck protested that a certain statement had been reported in the *House of Commons Debates*, the judge replied testily, "No, no, that is not permitted here, *Hansard* is not in this trial." In the almost uninterrupted stream of heckling from the bench, only one of the interruptions was to facilitate the proceedings. In that case the judge forgot himself for a moment and interjected, "There is no need to go into that, Mr. Sommerville, the crown counsel stated that they did not suggest that the Communist Party of Canada had anything to do with the Russian government or receives orders from the Russian government." One other judicial interjection evoked comment. Comrade Buck was drawing the attention of the jury to the program of unemployment relief and the party's bill for non-contributory unemployment insurance. The judge brought his hand down on his desk irritably and shouted, "Well, never mind that, *we* are not complaining about that." He couldn't have explained more clearly his identity with R. B. Bennett and the R.C.M.P. in the effort to convict the eight if he had made a whole speech.

In the circumstances the outcome of the trial was a foregone conclusion, The eight based their entire case upon the thesis stated in the following quotation from Buck's address to the jury:

"We do not believe that it is logical for intelligent men and women to think that a condition where millions and millions of people are starving should be allowed to prevail while warehouses are full of food. We do not believe that thousands of farmers and their families should starve because they cannot sell the food that they have grown. We do not believe that it is logical for intelligent men to assume that these things cannot be changed. But, we do understand that mere belief that they should be changed is not enough. They will not be changed by belief alone. Those members of the working class who want it must be organized to lead the whole of our class in overcoming the resistance of the capitalists.

"The working class cannot achieve that aim any more than it can successfully develop its immediate struggles against starvation and wage cuts, without its own revolutionary party, strong and disciplined, armed with working-class science That party is the Communist Party."[4]

The verdict Of the jury was "guilty." Mr. Justice Wright smacked his lips as he sentenced the seven members of the

Political Bureau of the party to five years' imprisonment for being members of an organization now declared illegal under the terms of Section 98, five years' imprisonment for being officers of that organization, and two years for having engaged in a seditious conspiracy to overthrow the capitalist state. Tom Cacic was sentenced only to the latter. (In keeping with the whole character of the trial, Cacic was not released when the Appeal Court nullified the "seditious conspiracy" count in the indictment. His two-year sentence was still considered to hold good and he went to Kingston Penitentiary with the others. The Bennett government deported Tom at the end of his sentence.)

* * *

The Attorney-General of Ontario boasted in a radio broadcast that "Communism will never raise its head in Ontario again." The party, now banned in Ontario, decided to test the validity of the attorney-general's statement. Pending the hearing of an appeal against their conviction, the eight comrades were freed on bail ($160,000) and Tim Buck was nominated for the Board, of Control in the Toronto municipal elections. To the surprise of the attorney-general and the reactionaries in general, 6,000 citizens of Toronto voted for Tim on January 1st. Small though the number appears today, it created a sensation at the time. It was more than double the highest vote ever cast for a candidate of the Communist Party in the city of Toronto up to that time. It was unquestionably a protest against the flagrant use of the courts to suppress political ideas.

The appeal was dismissed by five the Court of Appeals and the eight party leaders went to prison. Their incarceration did not reduce the effectiveness of the party's strugle, although outlawry of the party under Section 98 compelled a change in the forms of activity. The great crisis was at its most acute stage, with factories closing every day. Hundreds of thousands of workers were being unceremoniously discharged; those remaining at work suffered drastic wage cuts. There was no unemployment insurance. As noted in an earlier chapter, 12,000 eviction orders were served in the Toronto area during the year in which the party was outlawed. Retail sales declined to only sixty per cent of what they had been in 1929.

Economic chaos prevailed throughout Canada and the United States, throughout the capitalist world in fact. Unemployment, hunger and hopelessness was the lot of millions of Canadians. Small business people were going bankrupt in thousands, farmers were losing their farms. In striking contrast to the utter chaos of capitalist economy, Soviet economy continued to expand. Visitors to the Soviet Union, of whom there were a great many, were returning with glowing reports of great new undertakings, of big new cities springing up in places where there had been no settlement before, of the rapid and uninterrupted increase in the number of workers employed in industry, of the demand for engineers, chemists, doctors, scientific workers, technicians and skilled craftsmen, which continued to grow even faster than the continually expanding educational facilities could train them. The contrast became so evident and so striking that it even broke through the conspiracy of silence maintained until then by the lying capitalist press. One by one capitalist papers, which were fighting for circulation started to publish occasional reports of the continued expansion of Soviet economy and the continued rise in the standard of living of the workers and farmers throughout the Soviet Union. Up went the circulation of such papers. The workers and farmers of Canada wanted to know about the society in which there was no fear of economic crisis.

Canadian workers reacted vigorously against the putting of Hitler in power by the German capitalists after his second defeat at the polls. Canadian workers saw in the tactics of the German imperialists the pattern being developed by monopoly-capital throughout the capitalist world. In Toronto a powerful anti-Hitler parade, concluding with a great anti-fascist demonstration in Queen's Park, showed the mass anti-fascist sentiment of the working people and the fact that growing and increasingly militant democratic action was forcing the police to

86

back down from their attempt to prohibit mass public activities of a genuinely working-class character.

Realization grew that the economic crisis was not an unavoidable natural disaster. Somewhat later, there was extending realization that, even with the economic crisis, it would have been physically quite a simple matter for the government to have taken measures to ensure food, fuel, and other elementary necessities for the people, to have protected small homeowners and farmers. The Unemployed Workers' Associations became mass movements. "Hunger Marches" to city halls, to provincial legislatures, to Ottawa, forced the provincial and federal governments to accept a share of the cost of relief.

It became evident that, while small business people were getting it in the neck, monopoly-capital was maintaining its profits by intensifying its exploitation of the workers. There developed bitter resentment against the manner in which big business was actually increasing its rate of profit by exploiting the plight of the masses of the people. The Bennett government was compelled to set up a royal commission to investigate "Cost-Spreads and Mass Buying." Evidence brought out before this commission revealed horrible conditions in important sections of Canadian industry and commerce. Girls were working fifty-four hours per week for $9.00. Married men worked a fifty-four-hour week for $15.00, in some cases for even less. The big chain store and departmental store corporations were forcing down the prices paid to small manufacturers to a point at which, despite merciless wage-cutting and exploitation of their workers, some small manufacturers went bankrupt even while their factories were operating at a high level.

The revelations, concerning the profits of big business and the manner in which finance-capitalist enterprises were exploiting the crisis sharpened the resentment of the farmers. The Farmers' Unity League developed a wide popular campaign.

Across the country, the Workers' Unity League initiated a

great mass campaign in support of the unemployed workers. The bill for national unemployment insurance for which the party and the W.U.L. had collected 100,000 signatures during 1931 became the unofficial program of one million Canadians supported by hundreds of thousands of those who were still employed. In Montreal a mighty demonstration of 15,000 unemployed workers compelled the reactionary city council to change its policy. Their organization, l'Association Humanitaire, achieved a membership of 7,000.

Gideon Robertson who, as minister of labor in the Tory Union government had smashed the Winnipeg Strike in 1919, became minister of labor again in the Tory "Iron Heel" government of R. B. Bennett. When Robertson visited Winnipeg in 1932, six thousand workers under the leadership of party and Y.C.L. organizers Charlie Marriott and Norman Freed met him at the railway station with the slogan: "A Faker Comes to Town," and a powerful demonstration against both his treacherous role in Winnipeg in 1919 and the policies that hee then represented.

The local councils of unemployed workers became the rallying centres for a large section of the trade union movement as well as for unemployed workers. The councils made certain that the families of unemployed workers were fed. So effective did their fight on this issue become that local welfare departments tended increasingly to grant relief to families upon the demand of the unemployed workers' councils. The councils organized "round-the-clock" mass pickets upon request to defend workers against threatened eviction.

No conditions were attached to their assistance. Defence was organized for the homes of workers who had never been near the council as promptly as for its most active members. In struggles to defend the most elementary human rights of the working class, in actions which ranged from securing milk for babies to protecting a family from eviction and organizing hunger marches to the provincial capitals and to Ottawa, the local councils of unemployed workers brought forward a whole new generation of gifted, militant, working-class leaders whose work has continued to enrich the trade union and general labor movement. It is impossible to name all those comrades or even enough of them to be truly representative but they were typified by our comrades George Harris, Bob Haddow, Harvey Murphy, Harry Bell, Fred Collins, Tom (later Alderman) Raycraft, Mitchell Sago, Bob Kerr, the late Arthur (Slim) Evans, Malcolm MacLeod, and Hughie Anderson. There are scores of others of whom specific note is precluded by considerations of space.

While defending the elementary interests of the working class through its leadership of the unemployed workers, the W.U.L. rallied the workers who were still employed. Mass resistance was organized against wage cuts, the lengthening of hours and the merciless speed-up by which the bosses were taking wholesale advantage of the crisis. Organizational campaigns were carried through successfully in the midst of crisis and mass unemployment. With very limited forces and no central treasury, dependent entirely upon, the moral, financial and organizational support of the labor movement, the W.U.L. generated and led nation-wide resistance which stopped the wage cuts. In the process the W.U.L. organized a hundred thousand workers in industries that had never been organized before. Several of its strikes will stand for a long time as historic examples of working-class action. The great strike of the longshoremen in Montreal, led by rank-and-file workers, defied the combined forces of the bosses and the municipal and provincial governments. Stratford, where workers never previously organized maintained their mass picket line in defiance of troops and tanks.. Frazer Mills, where the strike was carried through "looking into the muzzles" of machine guns. Noranda, where militancy aroused neighboring bushworkers to drop their axes and take their places in the miners' picket line. Corbin, where striking miners and their families held out for five months against police and mine-company violence -- and called off the strike only after the company completely abandoned the mine. True, there were victims of employer viciousness and police violence -- Nick Zenchuk shot in the back by a policeman in Montreal while being evicted; three miners shot dead and thirteen wounded by volleys from the rifles of Mounties shooting up a peaceful and lawful joint meeting of striking miners in Estevan; brutal organized violence at Flin Flon, at Anyox, every place where workers struggled -- but organization went on. The long-established tradition of the A.F.L. that "workers can't be organized in hard times" was shown to be false. The number of strikes increased. In all Canada there were 86 strikes in 1931 and the number increased steadily to 189 in 1934. Of the 189 in 1934, no less than 109 were fought under the leadership of the Workers' Unity League and of those, 84 were won. The only strikes won by the workers during the crisis years were led by the W.U.L.

It was in the conditions which culminated in the events described above that the Canadian Labor Defence League carried through its campaign for the repeal of Section 98 and release of the eight Communists. Popular resentment against the policies of the Bennett government helped the C.L.D.L. campaign. Its national petition for' the repeal of Section 98 and the release of the eight Communists was signed by 483,000 Canadians. Whole municipal councils signed it, the entire membership of local unions and the entire working force in some mines and camps. Public interest in the question was extended as a result of the fact that it became interwoven with the contest between the Liberals and the Tories for parliamentary support, with Mackenzie King seizing every opportunity to condemn Section 98 and R. B. Bennett's infringements of bourgeois democracy.

Added point was given to the intermingling of interests by the aftermath of the riots in Kingston Penitentiary in October, 1932. The causes of the riots were the medieval system of repression which characterized the penal system at that time, bad food and barbarous corporal punishment, sometimes for trivial offences. The Bennet government, however, thought it saw in the riots an opportunity to justify its persecution of the Communist

Party. Instead of recognizing the necessity for far reaching penal reform, the government sought to dismiss the protest actions of the inmates (none of whom sought to escape) as "trouble created by the Communists." The superintendent of penitentiaries, a recently appointed Tory friend of Bennett, wrote an utterly fantastic official explanation for the disturbances. According to him, the trouble was due solely to the fact that the Communists were so infernally clever that, even in the conditions. of repression which characterized Kingston Penitentiary at that time, they had succeeded in organizing the inmates to "overthrow the government."

In the manner characteristic of reactionaries, the Bennett government sought to make political capital of the "prison riot." Tim Buck was accused of fomenting and leading it. His ankles shackled with short chains to prevent him from taking steps of more than a few inches, and each hand handcuffed to the wrist of a guard on either side of him, preceded and followed by guards carrying loaded rifles at the ready, Tim Buck was taken into Kingston to stand trial amid elaborate pretences that the government feared an armed attempt to free him. But, again, the government's scheme boomeranged. Buck's defence in court was a frank statement that he had participated with the other convicts in a protest demonstration and he described the reasons why. His address exploded the fantastic "report" of the superintendent of penitentiaries. Combined with the fact that it became known that an attempt had been made by penitentiary officers to murder Tim Buck, the trial inclined reasonable people to the opinion that some sort of investigation was necessary. The government's attempts to use the prison riots to discredit the Communists boomeranged upon the government itself. The judgment rendered by Mr. Justice LaRoche tended to discredit the government still further. The judge pointed out that Buck's own statement "that he had left his place of work along with the other convicts in the machine shop as part of the protest action that the convicts were carrying out," made it incumbent upon the court to declare Buck guilty of the crime with which he had been charged. Buck had participated in a breach of discipline in the course of which property had been damaged or destroyed. The judge intimated, however, acknowledgment that the conditions in the penitentiary clamored for reform. Without actually using the words, he indicated strongly that in his opinion the convicts had a case. He acknowledged that provocation had been used. He had personally verified evidence of the attempt to shoot Buck in his cell. The judge demonstrated that he meant what he had said by sentencing Buck to one year, to be served concurrently. (The law under which Buck was charged provided a maximum sentence of fourteen years.)

During this same period the general secretary of the C.L.D.L., Comrade A. E. Smith, was arrested and charged with sedition, in an attempt to outlaw the C.L.D.L. The circumstances of his arrest and trial illustrated both the length to which the authorities were prepared to go in their efforts to suppress the popular movement, and the growing temper of the opposition to R. B. Bennett's "iron heel" policies. In the course of an address delivered in the Standard Theatre in Toronto, Comrade A. E. Smith had charged R. B. Bennett with the responsibility for the attempt to murder Tim Buck. He was promptly arrested and charged with sedition. The trial became a national issue. A prominent liberal lawyer, E. J. McMurray, K.C., of Winnipeg, defended Comrade Smith. Prominent representatives of the bar who had recently attended the famous Dimitroff trial in Leipzig selected one of their number to attend the Smith trial. A. E. Smith himself was a worthy Canadian counterpart of George Dimitroff in his bearing in the witness box. He did not retract a word. When Mr. McMurray demanded that Tim Buck be brought from Kingston to testify as a witness for the defence, the crown prosecutor and the court were in a frenzy. Every obstruction short of actually over-riding the letter of the law was resorted to in their effort to prevent the appearance of Tim Buck in that court. McMurray, however, would not be denied. Having held the office of attorney-general in the federal government, he was not to be stymied by their lawyers' tricks. Despite all their machinations, he gained his point and Tim Buck was brought from Kingston Penitentiary to Toronto.

Smuggled in irons from the penitentiary to the train at Kingston Junction and from the train, via the baggage room, to the Don Jail in Toronto, Buck was placed in, the debtors' room there to prevent any contact with other prisoners. Only one guard was allowed access to him. Meals were brought to the room and Buck was allowed exercise in the yard during the evening when lie could not be observed by other inmates. Everything possible was done to ensure that he should receive no word about the course of the trial during the three days that he was held there. Fortunately, one of the guards in the institution rebelled at the manner in which the authorities were trying to secure a conviction against Comrade A. E. Simth. One evening, shortly after supper, somebody outside the door whispered, "Are you in there, Tim Buck?" On being assured he said, "You'll have to be very careful, Tim, they are out to get Mr. Smith and they won't let you have your say if they can help it. I've written down the words that Smith used so you'll know what it is all about. I'm going to pass it through your ventilator. Promise you'll tear it up and put it down the can right away." With that he threw a note and a newspaper clipping wrapped around a tiny piece of coal through the small square opening over the door. On the note were written the words attributed to Smith; the newspaper clipping dealt with the controversy in court over whether Buck should be permitted to testify.

Thus warned, Buck was able to orientate himself. He decided that, in the circumstances, the important thing for him to do was to ensure that Comrade Smith's statement should be verified. He decided that no matter what should be the first question asked him, his answer should tell the jury that a deliberate attempt had been made to murder him. He spent the rest of his waiting time formulating the shortest possible answers to the various questions that might be asked first. When, eventually, he was placed in the witness box and the preliminaries had been completed, the first question put to him was: "Please tell the court what happened in the penitentiary on October 17, 1932." Instead of starting with the riot, Tim Buck quickly said, "I was shot at!" He was just in time; in fact, he had to speak loudly to make himself heard over the objections of the crown prosecutor. Buck was removed from the court and the defence did not succeed in getting him back. But the important evidence had been given and nothing the prosecution could do undid its effect. The jury brought in a verdict of "not guilty." Comrade A. E. Smith was free again to continue his leadership of the great national campaign for the release of the eight party leaders and the repeal of Section 98.

During this period and as part of the development typified by the A. E. Smith trial, the defiant warning of the eight leaders at the time of their conviction was being proved correct. In the name of the eight, Tim Buck had declared in court and at every meeting that he addressed in the municipal election campaign their complete confidence that "for every one of us being sent to prison, nine new younger and better working-class leaders will come forward." Following the Smith trial the correctness of that prophecy became evident. Membership in the Canadian Labor Defence League was increasing at the rate of more than a thousand every month. Its official organ, *Labor Defence*, had a circulation of 40,000 per issue. The party was outlawed, ten thousand workers had been arrested for working-class activities, scores had been convicted under Section 98 and imprisoned, hundreds had been deported to the British Isles and other countries. In spite of that, and the repeated declarations of the prime minister that "agitators and agitation will be crushed beneath an iron heel of ruthlessness," the party was growing faster than ever before in its history, as were the Workers' Unity League and the Y.C.L. When provincial elections were held in Ontario in 1934, the Tories suffered a resounding defeat and the

Liberals came to power in that province for the first time in a generation. It was clear that popular resentment against the Bennett policies was being ridden by the Liberal Party.

* * *

By June, 1934, the pressure of public opinion compelled the Bennett government to make some concessions. On June 12th, two of the party leaders were released from Kingston. Instead of their release taking the edge off the campaign as the Bennett government had assumed, it raised the campaign to a still higher level. From then onward party leaders were released one by one until the last one, Tim Buck, was set free on November 24. Within a few days of his release a special meeting of the party leadership was convened to consider immediate action. Because the party was outlawed and their release had no effect upon Section 98, the conference was held underground. It was agreed unanimously that the two most immediate tasks confronting the party were to bring about the widest possible democratic unity in the fight against the conditions of the crisis and, simultaneously, to smash the ban imposed upon the party under Section 98. It was decided that Buck, who had been released on parole and forbidden to participate in any public activities, should announce the party's decision to defy Section 98 at a mass meeting to welcome his release. That plan was carried out. Before 17,000 Toronto workers, gathered at the Maple Leaf Gardens and hundreds of R.C.M.P., provincial and municipal policemen, Tim Buck announced that the party intended to defy the ban and to "make Section 98, and the government's attempt to enforce it, ridiculous from end to end of Canada." From that meeting Comrade Buck went on a national tour during which he and local party leaders everywhere called upon great working-class meetings to defy the ban and force its removal. No action was taken against any person throughout the campaign. The, Bennett government couldn't use Section 98 again; it was discredited in the eyes of the people. By June of 1936 the King government, fresh from its victory in the election of October, 1935, repealed

Section 98 -- the Communist Party of Canada had regained legality.

Note

1. Lenin, "The Third International and Its Place in History," *Selected Works* Vol. 10, pp, 35-36.

2. The trials of the Winnipeg strike leaders did not involve the rights of a long-established public political party. They were tried, nominally at least, for what they were charged with having done; not for their opinions.

3. Gordon K. Sommerville, K.C.

4. *An Indictment of Capitalism.* Tim Buck's address to the jury, published by the Canadian Labor Defence League, p. 61.

CHAPTER SEVEN: A New Stage of Political Development

WHEN Mr. Justice Wright sentenced its leaders to imprisonment in November, 1931, the Communist Party of Canada was ten years old. It had led every progressive current in the Canadian labor movement throughout those ten years. Indeed, with the sole exception of the Canadian Labor Party, the Communists had initiated all the progressive movements and organized the early activities in support of them. Our party initiated and led to success the struggle against the ivory-tower sectarian isolation from the masses of the workers that had characterized the Socialist Party of Canada. Our Party initiated and led to victory the nation-wide campaign against the tradition of secession which had made two eneyations of militant workers politically sterile. In place of the false theory that secession from the craft unions was the hallmark of militancy, our party had won recognition of the fact that the place for a militant worker is in the union that is genuinely supported by the masses of his fellow-workers. The great "back-to-the-unions" movement led by our party had healed the catastrophic O.B.U. split and re-united the labor movement. Our party, along with the Trade Union Educational League and later the Workers' Unity League, had initiated and led the struggles for industrial unionism and to organize the unorganized. By its consistent battle for the Canadian Labor Defence League, our party had won recognition throughout the working-class movement of the necessity for organized labor defence.

The political advance that the working class made in those struggles was not always evident at the time. When the advance did become evident it appeared to be scattered. Basically, however, those progressive activities worked a profound change in the labor movement. Step by step the Communists led the

97

progressive workers forward along the historic path of working-class political development to mass understanding of the fact that, created by modern industry as a class by itself, the working class must become a class *for* itself; that the working class must consciously engage in the struggle to raise itself up from the position of an oppressed and exploited class to the position of the leading, ruling class in society.

Along with its fight for labor unity and independent working-class political action the party had initiated activities which mobilized tens of thousands of farmers on the Prairies in organized struggle against the ruthless exploitation of monopoly-capital and the cynical disregard of Liberal and Tory governments. The campaign led by the party and the Farmers' Unity League halted the ruthless sweep of foreclosures, sheriffs' sales and evictions. In the process it raised farmers' action on the Prairies to a new high level, arousing tens of thousands of poor farmers to recognition of the need for united farmer-labor political action.

The organization of unemployed workers on a national scale by the Workers' Unity League, the co-ordination of their struggles for survival and the great campaign for the Party's National Non-Contributory Unemployment Insurance Bill, were reaching a new high level when the Bennett government loosed the nation-wide R.C.M.P. raids and attempted to stamp out the growing radicalization of the workers and farmers by the use of the courts. The government failed to accomplish its purpose, however. It was precisely when capitalist law was exposed as an instrument for the suppression of working-class ideas and activities that the accumulated ideological results of the preceding decade of party work crystallized. Popular revulsion against the fascist methods of the Tory governments and the catastrophic effects of the economic crisis combined to create a situation characterized by the fact that the Canadian Labor Defence League secured 483,000 signatures to its second petition for the release of the eight Communists and repeal of Section 98.

This is not to suggest that all the people who signed the C.L.D.L. petition necessarily agreed with the Communist Party. A large number of them certainly did agree with the growing demand for a national program of great public works, to employ 200,000 Canadians improving Canada, and the demand for such a program had been initiated by our party. But, the decisive fact in connection with the enormous number of people who supported the C.L.D.L. petition was that they illustrated the widespread and acute dissatisfaction with the Tory government; indeed, those signatures testified to the measure in which elements of disintegration were developing within the two old parties of the capitalist class.

The Communist Party being outlawed, bourgeois politicians and social reformists seized upon the possibility presented by the widespread radicalization of workers, farmers and urban middle-class people.

During the year after the Bennett government banned the Communist Party, a conference of social democrats and leaders of farm organizations, held in Calgary, planned the organization of a new reformist party. Shortly afterwards H. H. Stevens, the minister of trade and commerce in Bennett's cabinet, utilized the popularity he had achieved by his sponsorship of the inquiry into cost-spreads and mass buying to organize a political party of his own, under the name of the National Reconstruction Party. Simultaneously, there emerged in Alberta a provincial party under the name and pretending to the philosophy of Social Credit. In the Province of Quebec, Paul Gouin, the son of Sir Lomer Gouin, long-time Liberal boss in that province, split the provincial Liberal Party and organized a movement of dissidents under the name of L'Action Liberale. Gouin pretended to progressive aims but in effect, the function of L'Action Liberale was to provide the means whereby some Quebec "Liberals" could merge with Duplessis.

In the federal elections held during October, 1935, more than a million of those who went to the polls voted for candidates other than those of the Liberal and Tory parties. Because the disintegrating influences affected mainly the Tory party, the Bennett government was the loser and the Liberals were returned to power.

The actual competition between Liberals and Tories in that, as in all elections, was solely as to which party could serve Canadian capitalism best. There was no difference in their attitudes towards the profit system. Such superficial difference as appeared between the attitude of the two parties towards the working class was the difference between Bennett's practice of the "iron heel" and King's promise of a velvet glove. At the same time, the defeat of the Bennett government was a setback for the most reactionary forces in Canada and the fact that a million (twenty-two percent) of all those who voted opposed both old parties was a serious warning to the victorious Liberals. Mackenzie King's repeal of Section 98 during the first session of the new parliament was a tacit admission of that fact. The monopoly of the two old parties had been broken: the new government was, for the time being at least, compelled to listen to the voice of the people.

* * *

Because the C.C.F. marked the establishment of a national social-democratic party politically identical with the social-democratic parties in Europe, its foundation was of special importance to the working class and, therefore, to the Communist Party.

It was a very important stage of the historic struggle of the workers and poor farmers to free themselves from the political tutelage of the capitalist class. Objectively the emergence of the C.C.F. was a result of the work of the Communist Party -- indeed it testified to the effectiveness of its work. Dialectically it was an integral part of the evolutionary process in which the working class learns by its own experience that *only its own party, based unequivocally upon the historical destiny of the working class, will lead it to victory.*

A very large proportion of the men and women who participated in the foundation of the C.C.F. had that process in mind at the time -- a much larger proportion than is generally realized. That they supported the establishment of a social-democratic party, the leaders of which refused to identify it directly with the aim of socialism, does not contradict their general socialist aspirations. In the conditions prevailing in Canada at that time, and the level of political development corresponding as it did with the relative youth of Canadian capitalism, it was inevitable that the first mass popular breakaway from capitalist politics should be of such a character. The fact that, turning away from the Liberal and Conservative parties, they established a radical reform party which "extended its hand," as it were, to the masses of workers who aspired to a socialist re-organization of Canada, made the foundation of the C.C.F. a development of tremendous importance. The law of working-class political growth makes it a stage in the advance of the working class to recognition of the historical necessity for Communist policies.

Along with large numbers of socialist-minded workers and farmers the foundation of the C.C.F. attracted wide circles of reform-minded people who, without definitely supporting socialism, recognized some of the evils of capitalism and wanted action to mitigate them. The Communist Party of Canada wanted to cooperate with all such democratic people even if such cooperation had to be limited only to the amelioration of the most pressing, immediate effects of the crisis. The Communist Party was fighting for what the majority of them aspired to. The attitude of the Party towards the C.C.F. movement was stated on behalf of the National Committee of the Party by Tim Buck in a public address delivered in Massey Hall in Toronto, early in 1935, to open the party's campaign for the federal general elections to be held that year. In the course of his address, Tim Buck explained the attitude described above, and appealed to the

C.C.F. leadership and members to join in a united front effort to ensure one labor or farmer candidate in each constituency in the forthcoming election. He pointed out that the conditions created by the splits in the old parties and the organizations of the new ones made it possible that an electoral united front of the C.C.F. and the Communist Party could rally the farm and labor movements to such an extent as to elect a farmer-labor government.

In addition to public proposals for electoral cooperation the Communist Party addressed a letter to the C.C.F. leadership setting forth specific proposals for an exchange of views concerning the possibility of cooperation and the means by which it could be made effective. The National Council of the C.C.F. rejected the proposal for electoral cooperation; instead it plunged into a campaign of violent propaganda against the C.P., the Soviet Union and all proposals that suggested a united front against monopoly capitalism. All its efforts to bring about electoral unity being rejected by the C.C.F. leadership, the Communist Party entered the federal elections with its own candidates and election platform. To limit electoral conflict between the party and the C.C.F. as much as possible, only nine candidates were nominated. The party's federal election program, of which 150,000 copies were distributed, was built around the following eight points:

> *THE COMMUNIST ELECTION PROGRAM*
> 1. Immediate enactment of genuine unemployment and social insurance at the expense of the rich, as embodied in the *Worker's Bill,* pending which unemployed relief to be paid at the rates of benefit provided in this bill.
> 2. To prevent further attacks upon the living standards of the masses, rising prices resulting from monopoly and inflation, wage cuts, relief cuts; to abolish sweat-shops and forced labor; to win higher wages, shorter hours, and improved working conditions. To prohibit all evictions and forced sales of workers' homes for debts or arrears in taxes. To prevent the railway amalgamation scheme of big

capital.

3. Repeal of the Natural Products Marketing Act and the Farm Creditors' Arrangement Act. Provision of emergency relief for all needy and drought-stricken farmers. Long-term farm credits at low interest. Cancellation of mortgages and debts of impoverished farmers. Prevention of the forced sale of farms, the seizure of crops and the forced collection of rent and taxes. Immediate enactment of the Farm Emergency Bill.

4. Repeal of Section 98. No utilization of police and militia against struggles of workers and farmers. Prevention of the deportation and oppression of foreign-born workers. Prevention and repeal of all measures restricting trade union rights. Prohibition of company unions. Maintenance of the right of workers to join the union of their choice, to strike, to picket and demonstrate without restriction. Immediate release of all workers imprisoned for labor activities.

5. Prevention by united mass struggle of the imperialist designs to hurl the Canadian masses into the imminent imperialist war. Prevention of the shipment of war materials to Japan and Germany. Against all war preparations and the war provocations of Canadian imperialism against the Soviet Union. Establishment of full diplomatic and trade relations with the Soviet Union. Support of the Soviet Union's peace policy. Defence of the Soviet Union and Soviet China[1] against imperialist attacks.

6. Immediate payment of all veterans' pensions, restoration of cancelled pensions, and free medical attention for all veterans.

7. Abolition of the sales tax; abolition of all taxes on necessities of life and on persons or the property of persons earning less than $3,000 per year; steeply graduated taxation on the rich.

8 Cancellation of the war-and-forced-labor building

program of the Bennett government; commencement of a billion-dollar building program at trade union wages, to clear the slums, build workers' homes, schools, hospitals and other works for the workers and farmers.

The party's proposal for electoral cooperation with the C.C.F. was reiterated in the following words:

"The Communist Election Committee proposes a united front of the C.C.F. and the Communist Party in the coming federal elections on the basis of the common economic and political interests of the masses in this fight. The Communist Election Committee calls for unity in struggle for the needs of the masses -- unity against the Liberal and Conservative parties of big capital -- unity for the election of a substantial number of Communist and C.C.F. candidates, who are pledged to the line of daily, united struggle against hunger, fascism and war."

The aggregate vote cast for the party's candidates in the elections was 21,000. Its significance was greater than its numbers, however. The party was illegal, the electorate was subjected to systematic anti-Communist propaganda, the C,C.F. leaders and most of the C.C.F. candidates exerted more efforts against the party than against the capitalist parties. While seeking to bring about a united front between the Communist Party and the C.C.F. it was necessary, during the infancy of the C.C.F., as today, for the Communist Party to carry on a consistent struggle against the illusion that the battle against monopoly-capitalism can be won by the policies and the methods pursued by the leadership of the C.C.F. Then as now it was necessary to expose and combat the anti-working-class ideology of the C.C.F. leaders. The "organized confusion" of their policies and propaganda tended to delude uncritical supporters into the idea that it was some sort of a new, easy, Canadian path to socialism. They calculatingly sidetracked the majority of delegates in the constituent convention from proclaiming socialism to be its goal. They aimed to make of the C.C.F. a revival of the opportunistic petty-bourgeois social reformism that had marked labor parliamentarism up to the end of the First World War, to make it the third party of bourgeois politics in Canada -- sharing the parliamentary field with the two old parties. The source of that aim and the consequent role played by the C.C.F. leadership since, of a buffer between the working class and the capitalist class, was fully explained at the time of its foundation by Stewart Smith in his book *Socialism and the C.C.F.*[2]

Even if Stewart Smith's book had never been written, the keynote speech submitted to the Regina convention by J. S. Woodsworth was full and conclusive evidence of the determination of its sponsors that the C.C.F. should not be a working-class party, and that it should not be committed to the aim of socialism. To mollify the large and enthusiastic left wing at the convention, Mr. Woodsworth explained his opposition to the word "socialism" or "socialist" in the name of the new party as follows: "Socialism has so many variations that we hesitate to use the class name." In the rest of his speech, he made it quite definite that the reason for not including the word socialism was not the "variations" but its class meaning. The dominant group at the foundation of the C.C.F. repudiated the word "socialism" precisely because it had become identified with the aspirations of the working class.

J. S. Woodsworth, whose memory is honored by the working-class movement because of his loyalty to progressive principles as he understood them, did not misrepresent his position. His aim was a reform party -- a party which could secure support from sections of the capitalist class, from well-to-do farmers and urban middle-class people, and from some workers. He did not pretend that he advocated socialism. His political philosophy was summed up in the following sentences which he repeated hundreds of times: "The state should own and control certain essential public utilities. That is all."[3] He often used the terms "cooperation," "planning," "public ownership," as though they were all synonymous with socialism. He did not differentiate between public ownership such as that of the Canadian National Railways, which was established *solely* to guarantee an undiminishing flow of unearned income to the capitalist class at the expense of the masses of the people, and genuine public ownership, exemplified in the Soviet Union, which puts an end to unearned increment and assures that all the advantages of ownership accrue to the community. He even welcomed as "advance along socialistic lines,"[4] the report submitted to the government by Sir Lyman Duff, later chief justice of Canada, recommending amalgamation of the Canadian National Railways and the Canadian Pacific Railway in a manner that would have established a C.P.R. monopoly of railroad transportation.

The real character of that proposal was described in the condemnation of it published by the Central Committee of the Communist Party, characterized by the following quotation:

> "Our country stands before a new attack on the welfare of the people. Powerful financial and industrial interests headed by Sir Edward Beatty, president of the C.P.R., are preparing to fasten a gigantic railroad monopoly on the people of Canada.
> "The proposals of Sir Edward Beatty are being supported by the reactionary press all over Canada. Cynical admissions are made by Sir Edward Beatty to the effect that the unification of the two railway systems will mean a reduction of staff, Every honest observer admits that if unification goes through to its final aim, complete amalgamation, from 30,000 to 40,000 railway workers will be discarded.
> "The Communist Party, through its Dominion Committee now in session, declares its complete accord with the railway unions, and great sections of the Canadian people, in saying: *This reactionary plot against the Canadian people must be foiled!.*"

Mr. Woodsworth stated his attitude towards finance-capital in the following words: "We are not advocating the immediate taking over of the banks, but we are advocating a central bank which will control credit and currency. This will prevent credit being extended at one time when it is not needed, and refused at times, like these, when it is urgently needed."[5]

How little of socialism there was in that proposal of the leader of the C.C.F. was proved two years later when the Tory government, headed by the crass reactionary Bennett, established a central bank, the Bank of Canada, to perform exactly the functions that Mr. Woodsworth had advocated as a solution for all financial ills. Unfortunately for the workers and farmers and small-business people, it gave no protection whatsoever to them. Contrary to the easy but unfounded assurances given by Mr. Woodsworth, it facilitated the extension of credit when that suited monopoly-capital, and it ensured even more drastic curtailment of credit and consequent refusal when the need of small-business people was desperate. Contrary to the assurances of Mr. Woodsworth, the central bank provided protection only for the capitalist banking system.

That particular example of C.C.F. policies is especially important today because the national leaders of the C.C.F. have refused to learn from experience. They still reject the idea of nationalizing the banking system and its function of creating credit. Indeed, they have made repudiation of the aim of nationalizing the chartered banks an expressly written part of C.C.F. policy.

Mr. Woodsworth did not misrepresent his political creed but the more hard-boiled right-wing social democrats around him were, and are, frequently, less honest in their declarations. One of the most serious crimes committed against the Canadian working class has been their deliberate "behind the barn" cultivation of the lie that their term "cooperative commonwealth" is synonymous with socialism, while systematically pursuing policies which support monopoly-capitalism against the working class. Occasionally they qualify their pretence concerning the meaning of "cooperative commonwealth" by explaining that their aim is "Canadian socialism." By that trick they compound their treachery. They set the workers under their influence against socialism by instilling into their thinking the completely false idea that socialism is a matter of national taste instead of the abolition of capitalist exploitation. That sort of unprincipled deception is illustrated today by the contrast between the aims and policies to which the C.C.F. was supposedly dedicated by its *Regina Manifesto*, and the aims and policy to which it is committed in practice by its national leaders. For example, the *Regina Manifesto* declared:

> "We stand resolutely against all participation in imperialist wars.... Canadians must refuse to be entangled in any more wars fought to make the world safe for capitalism."

Such is the position which is presented to rank-and-file workers as the C.C.F. attitude towards peace and war. What is the real policy now being pursued by the national leadership? It is one of complete and unconditional support of the actions of the St. Laurent government in its preparation for an aggressive imperialist war - "to make the world safe for capitalism."

Note

1. Following the Great March of the Red Army, a hundred million people in China had established Soviet Governments in their districts.

2. *Socialism and the C.C.F.,* Contemporary Publishing Association, Montreal, February, 1934.

3. *Toronto Daily Star,* February 15, 1933. Quoted by Stewart Smith in *Socialism and the C.C.F.*

4. *House of Commons Debates.*

5. *Toronto Daily Star,* February 15, 1933. Quoted by Stewart Smith in *Socialism and the C.C.F.*

CHAPTER EIGHT: Working Class Unity Against Fascism and War

THE NINTH plenum of the party, held immediately after the federal elections in 1935, marked another vitally important turn in the work of the party. The seventh world congress of the Communist International had been held during July and August. At that historic gathering, George Dimitroff, the hero of Leipzig, had analyzed the meaning for all people of Hitler's accession to power in Germany. He had shown how the turn of monopoly-capitalism to policies aimed at fascism and war intensified the need for working-class unity in defence of democracy and peace. The report of the Canadian delegates to the congress was delivered at the ninth plenum by Comrade Stewart Smith, the chairman of the delegation. Quoting Dimitroff's historic report he pointed out that "the accession to power of fascism is not an *ordinary succession* of one bourgeois government by another, but a *substitution* of one state form of class domination of the bourgeoisie, bourgeois democracy, by another form -- open terrorist dictatorship . . . Before the establishment of a fascist dictatorship, bourgeois governments usually pass through a number of preliminary stages and institute a number of reactionary measures which directly facilitate the accession to power of fascism. Whoever does not fight the reactionary measures of the bourgeoisie and the growth of fascism at these preparatory stages, is not in a position to prevent the victory of fascism but, on the contrary, facilitates that victory."[1]

Comrade Smith pointed out that "the struggle for peace organized and led by the Communists, for example in France, had been decisive so far in saving the world from war.... The seventh congress of the Communist International repudiated the slander that the Communists would like to see war break out in the hope that it would bring revolution." It called upon all democratic forces to join with the Communists in defence of peace. To the question then being asked by widening circles of workers: "How can fascism be averted in the countries where it has not already come to power?" Dimitroff had announced firmly:

> "The first thing that must be done, the thing with which to commence, is to form a united front, to establish unity of action of workers in every factory, in every district, in every region, in every country, all over the world. Unity of action of the proletariat on a national and international scale is the mighty weapon which renders the working class capable not only of successful defence, but also of successful counter-offensive against fascism, against the class enemy."[2]

Stewart Smith proposed on behalf of the Political Bureau that the entire line of the party, all its activities, should be directed to the development of working-class unity. He signalized the unqualified character of the party's proposal for unity by announcing the willingness of the party to support the merging of the revolutionary unions of the Workers' Unity League in the A.F.L. and the C.I.O. In the name of the Political Bureau he declared: "By trade union unity, the working class and the revolutionary movement will lose nothing but will gain much greater strength than ever before. The revolutionary unions were formed solely because in the conditions then existing they were necessary to strengthen the working class. If, now, unity can be achieved then this is in line with the whole purpose and objective of the revolutionary unions and the Communist Party."[3]

The plenum directed the party membership towards a series of new tasks, each one designed to develop the struggle for labor and people's democratic unity all over Canada.

* * *

Following the plenum, every effort was made to eliminate barriers between various sections of the labor movement and united action for peace and democratic progress. The party supported the activities of the Canadian League Against War and Fascism which had recently been organized under the leadership of A. A. MacLeod on the inspiration of the magnificent Henri Barbusse. The party sought united action with workers and farmers on all issues of concern to Canadian democrats and placed no conditions upon its participation in such united actions.

The tactics indicated by the seventh congress of the Communist International corresponded exactly with the situation created in Canada by the militancy of the new and growing C.I.O. and its fight for industrial unionism. It was clear that the path by which Canadian workers could best make gains and strengthen their effectiveness as a class was through trade union unity.

The party concentrated even more energy upon the fight to build the new C.I.O. unions. It would require too much space and it is beyond the purpose of this work to record the contributions made by Communists to the establishment and building of the C.I.O. unions in Canada -- as in the United States. Their work in Canada was typified by our late beloved Dick Steele, national organizer for Canada of the Steel Workers' Organizing Committee, forerunner of the United Steel Workers of America. Dick Steele, with Harry Hunter, Harry Hambleton, George MacEachren and other Communists built up the foundation Canadian organization of what is now the Canadian District of the United Steel Workers.

The Canadian Seamen's Union was started in Toronto by a group of militant lake seamen, typified by Dewar Ferguson. Under the personal guidance of Joe Salsberg that group of militants reached out to the neighboring ports while they were still in the process of organizing the sailors in Toronto in preparation for the opening of navigation in the spring of 1936. Within a few years the C.S.U. transformed conditions of sailors on the Great Lakes. Before the C.S.U., sailors worked twelve hours per day seven days a week while sailing; the C.S.U. won them an eight-hour day and a forty-eight-hour week. While cutting their working hours per month in half, the C.S.U. raised the monthly pay of lake sailors from $35.00 to $40.00 minimum, with time and a half for all overtime worked over the eight contracted for in any one day. Before the C.S.U. the members of crews were completely at the mercy of vicious, and sometimes sadistic, first mates. Along with improved conditions the C.S.U. established the right of seamen to be dignified and responsible members of the community operating their ship, speaking as a collective through their union committee.

The party developed a powerful campaign among the revolutionary unions of the Workers' Unity League for their affiliation to the A.F.L. and the C.I.O. There was resistance from some of the unions. In some districts millitant workers considered the independence of their unions from the reactionary officialdom of the internationals as an immediate end in itself. In some industries bureaucratic international officers placed onerous conditions upon acceptance of the membership of the revolutionary unions. Some revolutionary trade unionists had become embittered and could not stomach the idea of "knuckling down" to the reactionaries.[4] But, within less than two years, the revolutionary unions were affiliated to the respective internationals -- the self-dissolution of the heroic Workers' Unity League was complete.

The party appealed to the members of the church. It called upon its own members everywhere to combat the lying propaganda by which the capitalist class was building a barrier of prejudice between workers who followed the leadership of the Communist Party and those who followed the leadership of the church.

In French Canada the party led by Fred Rose and the Y.C.L. led by Dave Kashtan had extended their hands with appeals addressed specifically to working men and women of the Catholic faith. Emphasizing the urgent need for united action in defence of the workers, small farmers and urban middle-class people against the effects of the economic crisis and the depredations of the "Trustards," the party and the Y.C.L. had

113

offered loyal and wholehearted cooperation in joint action, without regard to philosophical differences. Following that excellent example from Quebec, the plenum of the Central Committee declared in the name of the party as a whole:

> "Equally as in the struggle to develop trade union unity, our party is faced with the task of developing still further the friendly relations that exist between us and large numbers of church people.... There is a widespread misunderstanding at the present time that we ourselves do not always do enough to dispel. Many sincere Catholics believe that the main activity of the Communist Party is to fight the church. This misunderstanding is dangerous to the whole working-class movement. . . . It is a fact that there exists a section of the leadership of the church which tends to support forces making towards reactionary policies. . . . But Catholics, as such, are not against progress; they want progressive social legislation. It is because we ourselves have not sufficiently explained our position in this respect that we permit Catholics and Protestants, members of all churches, to believe the lying slander that the Communist Party is fighting against religious people. By that lie, the enemies of the working class and democracy are able to divert thousands of sincere people away from the struggle for progress."[5]

Enumerating examples of needs and interests shared by all sections of the working class regardless of political opinion or religious faith, the statement of the C.P. reminded members of the church that those common interests "are to be seen in practically all those wants and needs and hopes and fears which are common to the whole working class and which find expression in widespread poverty, unemployment, suffering of infants and fear of the future which comes of the general and growing insecurity of life under capitalism."[6]

One of the greatest achievements of the party during that period was the transformation of its twice-weekly paper, *The*

Worker, into the *Daily Clarion*. The change was more than a party achievement -- it was evidence of the growth of the united front. As the party declared in its national conference of 1936: "The measure of achievement that the establishment of a daily paper reflects is tremendous. It is not merely a manifestation of the increased strength of the revolutionary movement, but also of the broadening character of the labor movement as a whole. It reflects the fact that revolutionary workers no longer live to themselves in a narrow sect, but live, move and have wide influence in every phase of the labor movement."[7]

* * *

One of the truly historic landmarks in the accomplishments of the party during its fight for unity against fascism through the 1930's was its mobilization of all that was finest in Canadian democracy to support the democratic government of Spain.

It happened that a delegation of Canadian youth, representing the Youth Congress movement, was in Europe when the generals launched their military revolt against the newly-elected liberal government in Spain. Three of the young Canadians journeyed to Spain to see for themselves the character of the government and of the generals' revolution against it. They saw that it was a liberal government, headed by Senor Azana, a famous liberal constitutionalist. It was elected under the electoral law enacted by the conservative government that it defeated. They saw that it was supported by the overwhelming majority of the people while the rebelling generals were dependent upon aid from Hitler and Mussolini. In September, 1936, the general secretary of the party attended the Madrid discussions in which it was decided to appeal to world democracy to organize support for the Loyalist cause. Immediately upon his return to Canada, the party called for all-out aid to Spanish democracy.

Dr. Norman Bethune, a member of the party in Montreal, volunteered immediately to organize and head a field service blood transfusion unit. A national Committee to Aid Spanish Democracy was organized to sponsor and finance such a unit. The Rev. Ben Spence of the United Church, a prominent member of the Ontario Provincial Council of the C.C.F., was the first chairman of that committee. Its secretary was Norman Freed of the C.P. of Canada. The extent to which united action was being developed at that time is illustrated by the fact that the then provincial leader of the C.C.F. in Ontario, Graham Spry, was one of its vice-chairmen, Tim Buck the other. The committee included representatives of the Amalgamated Clothing Workers, the International Ladies' Garment Workers, the International Association of Machinsts, the Toronto and District Trades and Labor Council, the Women's League for Peace and Freedom, the League for Peace and Democracy, the Communist Party and numerous other organizations, both reformist and revolutionary.

Stimulated by the drive of Dr. Bethune and enthusiastic labor support, the blood transfusion unit was quickly organized and proceeded to Spain. The story of its work has been told elsewhere, but no history of the Communist Party of Canada would be complete without a tribute to the leader of that unit and those of his staff who served with it in Spain from the beginning to the end. It was their tireless energy, their courage and devotion that saw it through. The unit made medical as well as political history. It demonstrated for the first time in active service the possibility of storing blood and giving transfusions on the battlefield. Dr. Bethune died later, a hero's death, serving with the Chinese Red Army during its war against the Japanese invasion of China.

The other historic achievement of Canadian democracy, under the leadership of the Communist Party during that conflict, was the organization of the volunteer Canadian battalion which fought side by side with the representatives of democracy from all countries in the International Brigade. The 1,283 young Canadians who joined the Mackenzie-Papineau Battalion were not all members of the Communist Party or the Young

Communist League, but they were all heroes. They covered the name of Canada with glory, from Jarama to the Ebro, in the greatest battles fought against fascism in that war. Half of their number remained after the war, under the warm brown soil of Spain. Mourned by their comrades and their families, at the same time their sacrifice was a cause for pride -- it marked the maturity of true internationalism in Canadian democracy.

* * *

Maurice Duplessis won the provincial elections in Quebec in 1936 and became premier of that province. In March, 1937, he enacted his fascist, Padlock Law. Clearly the victory of the Liberal Party in the federal general elections of 1935 had not stopped the drive of the monopolists to policies of fascism and war. Indeed, as Fred Rose showed in his thoroughly documented booklet, *Hitler's Fifth Column in Quebec*, Duplessis' victory was part of the pattern of increasingly systematic support of the fascist trend by monopoly-capital. In addition Fred Rose made a startling exposè of the growing influence of fascist agents, representing the governments of both Hitler and Mussolini, in high places in Canada. He exposed the scheme by which those agents, the fascist organizations in Canada, big business, and influential Canadian politicians, all cooperated. Later, by calling public attention to the deal then being negotiated in secrecy, he compelled the federal government to take notice of the scheme which would have enabled Hitler to establish a German base on Anticosti Island -- in the Gulf of the St. Lawrence River.

During that period several open fascist organizations were launched in Canada. Some of those organizations were direct and evident imitations or subsidiaries of Hitler's Nazi party or Mussolini's Blackshirts. Such were the so-called "National Party", with headquarters at Winkler, Manitoba, and "The Blackshirts," associated with Catholic youth activities in several localities. Others, e.g., "The National Unity Party," and the fascist paper *Unite*, published by a subsidiary of the Catholic church in Quebec, were cunningly designed to give the impression of being spontaneous developments. All of the fascist organizations had one thing in common, however: they were lavishly financed from sources outside of their membership and they were encouraged openly by police and other governmental authorities -- including pressure from army officers upon their rank and file to attend fascist meetings in uniform.

But while monopoly-capital and its Tory politicians were fostering "hot-house" fascist organizations, the Communist Party's struggle for united labor action to defend democracy and, peace was arousing broad democratic action. When Hitler sent his warships, the Emden and the Karlsruhe, on a visit to Canada, masses of workers and democratic middle-class people in Montreal and Vancouver joined in the great anti-Nazi protest against the desecration of Canada's territorial waters by those sinister omens of fascism and its plans for war.

* * *

During that period, and definitely related to its emphasis upon united democratic action against the effects of the economic crisis and against the growing threat of fascism and war, the party made its first substantial steps in developing unity with and among important circles of artists and other activists on the cultural front in French and English-speaking Canada. The Progressive Arts Clubs, then the Progressive Theatre movement and the progressive dance groups, were the more evident and the newly organized expressions of that democratic advance on the cultural front, but they were only part of it. During that period, the tireless and long sustained work of comrades typified by Chris Daffef, bore fruit in numerous young artists at or near the top in their professions and in working-class choirs and orchestras which command the respect of the bourgeois critics. It was during that period that Avrom's work started to demonstrate the qualitative contribution that artists and cultural Workers in general can make, both to their art and to the working-class movement, by the complete integration of themselves and their striving for ever-more effective artistic expression in the struggle of the working class and its democratic allies.

Canada's first periodical devoted entirely to the fight for development of a people's culture was launched during that period. *New Frontiers* could not be maintained then, but the developments in which it played a fruitful part established the basis upon which its successor, the present *New Frontiers*, carries on.

As part of the general expansion of progressive cultural activities there was an important advance in the cultural work of the democratic mass organizations also. The Ukrainian Labor-Farmer Temple Association, which had organized choirs, orchestras, dance groups, drama groups, sports clubs, etc., in dozens of localities during the 1920's, now gave leadership to other democratic Slavic organizations, and organized inspiring large-scale festivals of folk culture. Their festival at the Mutual Street Arena, Toronto, in 1938, with more than 1,000 participants, was a cultural milestone of national importance. It was recognized as such in the reviews by the art critics of the capitalist press. The Finnish workers also developed their cultural activities on a higher scale during that period. In addition to their local bands, choirs, drama groups, sports clubs, etc., they developed their annual Sports Festival to a great annual national event which has continued to grow. The Toronto Jewish Folk Choir had not then achieved the superlative artistic level for which it is famous today but it, as the several other Jewish folk choirs across the country, became in that period an important factor in the extending battle for a Canadian people's culture.

Equally as important as the quantitative growth of progressive cultural activities during that period, was the two-sided development in which progressive cultural activists became inspired with a new and deeper understanding of the significance of the struggle to develop a Canadian people's culture, while at the same time reaching ever-wider audiences and thereby enriching and leavening the cultural life of Canada today. It is very largely as a result of their work that there is growing at last a

119

recognition of the fact that when an authentic Canadian national culture emerges, it will be more than the culture of the English, French, or any specific national group. It will be richer, more varied than any of them, because it will be made up of the best than can be contributed by each -- French, English, Slavic, Magyar, yes and North American Indian, etc. It Will be a higher culture; historically more advanced than any of its components because it will be synthesized only through consistent struggle to develop a truly Canadian culture in the face of the multi-million dollar outpourings of Hollywood and other cultural abattoirs of United States imperialism. Recognition of that fact and willingness to draw democratic conclusions from it is the decisive test of democratic bourgeois intellectuals of French and English-speaking Canada today. Failure to recognize it, or refusal to be guided by it, can only make cultural work un-Canadian and sterile.

* * *

The party's struggle for united action against the danger of fascism and war brought big changes in the labor movement during that period. We learned by our own experience that the fight for unity is a continuing struggle. In the course of it we improve our own understanding in the process of developing from primitive beginnings.

Most impressive demonstrations of the breadth of the united front achieved in that period were the great May Day parades and meetings. The parades, starting from various points, e.g. Riverdale Park, Dufferin Park, Stanley Park, marched across the city to converge at the University Avenue and College Street entrance to Queen's Park. On May Day, 1938, there were 22,000 marchers in the combined parade. The united front character of the demonstration is illustrated by the fact that the Rev. Ben Spence of the C.C.F. was regularly the elected chairman of the United Labor May Day Committee and Norman Freed of the Communist Party was, with equal regularity, elected secretary. United action in the trade union field was developed to a greater extent than at any time previously. The president of the Trades and Labor Congress of Canada (P. M. Draper) cooperated closely with the leading Communists in the trade union movement, joining whole-heartedly in their aim to secure a wider measure of Canadian autonomy. The rise of the New Democracy Movement, headed by W. D. Herridge, marked the high point of the movement that had developed looking to unity of all democratic forces in Canada. The thesis around which W. D. Herridge sought to unite the various groupings of the labor and farmer movements was expressed in the following, from his programmatic speech made to the young Conservatives:

> "Scarcity in the midst of plenty is becoming an affront to the intelligence of the man on the street....
> "To gain power, fascism makes trade unionism the public enemy. To retain power, fascism must destroy democracy in this modem form....
> "When fascism comes into power, trade unionism goes out....[8]

The attitude of the Communist Party towards the New Democracy Movement was stated by the eigth national convention of the party on October 8-13, 1937, as follows:

> "We, in common with all progressive people, welcome the sentiments expressed by W. D. Herridge in the address from which these quotations were taken. We will do all in our power to enable him and democratic elements in both capitalist parties to implement the anti-fascist position that he, there, sets forth."[9]
> "A powerful people's movement could compel King to impose special taxes upon the 'runaway' Canadian millionaires.... It could arouse the people against the scheme to give the C.N.R. to the Holt, Beatty, Bennett interests.
> "A wide popular movement could secure a comprehensive Dominion home-building scheme which would provide employment and eliminate slums. It could secure a

Dominion government rehabilitation fund to enable impoverished farmers to put their farms on an efficient producing basis.... It could influence King to establish friendly relations with the democratic government of Spain and to render aid to that beleaguered democracy. It could help to establish full trading relations between Canada and the U.S.S.R. . . . it could unite the great mass of the Canadian people of all shades of political opinion in its demand for the repeal of the Military Service Act."[10]

Unfortunately, however, the national leadership of the C.C.F. prevented any organized, democratic front at that time. Frightened by the increasing participation of C.C.F. members, the top leadership insisted upon the withdrawal of C.C.F. representatives from all such activities. Graham Spry, the Ontario leader, withdrew from the Committee to Aid Spanish Democracy. Prof. Underhill, one of the top "brain-trusters" of the C.C.F. leadership, announced that "the revolution is definitely off." The C.C.F. leadership did not decide on the basis of Prof. Underhill's analysis to disband; instead they decided to make their policies conform more closely with the aims of Canadian imperialism. They re-directed C.C.F. activities along the path which led in September, 1939, to the situation in which J. S. Woodsworth, alone, voted for the principles stated in the program of the C.C.F. against the government's proposal to take Canada into war. All the rest of the C.C.F. group voted with Canadian imperialism against the founder and leader of their own party.

Note

1. *Reports and Resolutions*, Ninth Plenum Communist Party of Canada, November, 1935.

2. *Reports and Resolutions*, Ninth Plenum C. P. of C., p. 13.

3. *Reports and Resolutions*, Ninth Plenum C. P. of C., p. 34.

4. The outstanding and most regrettable example was the great Jim MacLachlan. Jim disagreed with the idea of reuniting in the internationals. He fought against it even to the length of quitting the party to the building of which he had contributed so much.

5. *Towards a Democratic Front*, Tim Buck, p. 32.

6. *Towards a Democratic Front*, Tim Buck, p. 36.

7. *The Road Ahead*, Report to Eleventh Plenum, p. 75.

8. Quoted in *Monopoly vs. the People,* 1932. p. 32.

9. Monopoly vs. the People, p. 32.

10. *The Road Ahead,* Report to Eleventh Plenum, C. P. of C., 1937, p. 29.

CHAPTER NINE: Canada's youth Comes Of Age

AS POINTED out in an earlier chapter, the crisis and the depression brought both victimization of the youth and increasing militancy on their part. The degradation imposed on young workers as a result of the crisis almost defies description. The Dominion Bureau of Statistics admitted in 1936, that there were 200,000 unemployed males in urban communities between the ages of 15 and 24. The tens of thousands of unemployed youth who were classified as transients were not included, neither were the unemployed rural youth. The number of unemployed females of the same age groups was at least equal to the males, so it is evident that there were around half a million unemployed young men and women between the ages of 15 and 24. The conditions forced upon them were spotlighted by the fact that, during 1934, 40,000 of them could find no refuge other than the Bennett slave camps at twenty cents per day. Relief allowances granted to single girls were slashed again and again until girls were forced into degrading occupations. As the Young Communist League pointed out in its seventh national convention, August, 1934, "A whole generation is growing up that has never had a chance to earn a living and has only unemployment, hunger and misery as its perspective."

The revolt of the youth against those conditions was expressed in increasing participation of young workers in the militant struggles of the unemployed councils, in the militant unions led by the W.U.L. and in extending youth protest action. The Y.C.L. became the mobilizing force for widening circles of young workers in strike actions. In Stratford, Flin Flon, Noranda, Sault Ste. Marie, Fraser Mills, B.C., Timmins, Cochrane, Montreal, Winnipeg, etc., youth was in the forefront of the struggle. Leaders of the youth movement were frequently arrested and imprisoned. Many of them won national recognition as strike leaders.

As the crisis gave way to the long "depression of a special kind,"[1] with no prospect of re-employment for hundreds of thousands of workers, ever wider circles of democratic people recognized the criminal character of the treatment being meted out to Canada's youth. "Save Our Youth" became the slogan of millions of Canadians. So powerful was the pressure of youth desire for action to meet the conditions created by the crisis that even the upper hierarchy of the Catholic church was eventually compelled, unwillingly, to acquiesce in the participation of Catholic youth organizations in the great Youth Congress. The youth were in revolt against Bennett's slave camps. "Abolish the Slave Camps" became the slogan of the labor movement. When the youth marched out of the camps all over British Columbia and assembled in Vancouver, thousands of working-class homes were opened to them. They were housed and fed, often by sharing the family's relief rations. At the call of the heroic women members of the Communist Party in Vancouver, five thousand working-class women came out to a special "Mother's Day" demonstration on behalf of the camp workers and to demand the closing of the camps.

Recognizing that only action on a national scale could move the Bennett government, the British Columbia Provincial Committee of the party, with the officers of the W.U.L. and the Camp Workers' Union decided to undertake a great march, under the leadership of Comrade Arthur (Slim) Evans, across the country to Ottawa. When they left Vancouver 800-strong the capitalist class and its press sneered. They didn't believe the boys would stand tip to the bitter hardships of such an undertaking. "Wait until they feel the nip of frost up in the mountains" wrote one hack, "and they'll be glad to get back to camp." But he was wrong. The trekkers crossed the interior of British Columbia, crossed the Rocky Mountains, crossed most of the Prairies. They reached Regina in the third week of June. They had covered a thousand miles, half of their journey, *and their numbers had doubled*. They were completely confident of their ability to reach Ottawa and that their numbers would double again during the remainder of their journey.

In all the larger centres along their route reinforcements were gathering and preparing to join the trek. In Winnipeg alone there were hundreds waiting to join. The feeling was growing all over the country that this great national protest would compel the Tory government to close the slave camps.

The trekkers' amazing demonstration of discipline, no less than the unprecedented support that they received from the citizenry in every town that they passed through, provided conclusive evidence that the slave camps had to go. The Bennett government stopped the trek by the bloody massacre at Regina on Dominion Day, 1935, but they could not undo, what the young camp workers' trek had accomplished. Bennett's slave camps were discredited. The camp workers had marched out of Vancouver under the slogan "Abolish the Slave Camps." Not another camp was opened after the Regina massacre and within a few months not one remained in operation anywhere in Canada.

A revolutionary youth movement was built among the farm youth in over 100 communities across the Prairies. Young farm youth such as Bill Repka, Bill Halina, Bill Kardash, Ivan Birchard and others, became mass leaders by virtue of the support given by the youth to the struggles of the Farmers' Unity League.

A students' movement sprang up, with organizations in six universities and in high schools in virtually every city from Montreal west. The "Pioneers" movement of children extended to a membership of more than 6,000, publishing its own magazine with a circulation of more than 4,000. The official organ of the Y.C.L. *The Young Worker* was transformed from a monthly into a weekly with a growing circulation.

At the ninth plenum of the party, November, 1935, Bill

Kashtan, then secretary of the Y.C.L., projected a new conception of the role that the Y.C.L. should play. Reporting the gains made he emphasized the fact that, encouraging though they were, the gains lagged far behind the rising temper and the extending militancy of the Canadian youth. Reiterating that "the youth movement is the heart of the movement for social emancipation," Bill Kashtan called upon the party and the Y.C.L. to raise their sights and measure up to the needs of the youth. Advocating simultaneously a reorganization of the Y.C.L. along the lines of a more flexible educational youth organization, he charged it with the task of leading the masses of students, young workers and intellectuals, in an independent united front organization to defend the immediate interests of the youth. In the light of what was accomplished by the great Youth Congress movement, it is valuable now to quote the words in which Bill Kashtan projected the idea of it for the first time:

> "In general, I think we can work along the lines of building up a federation of youth organizations, on a platform of struggle for the immediate economic and political needs of the youth, against war and fascism, for socialism. Essentially such a federation would unite all youth prepared to stand on a working-class program, to work for the transformation of society. Such a federation could draw into its ranks the youth organizations which already exist in the working-class movement, unemployed youth organizations, student organizations, sports clubs, the Y.C.L. and probably also the Cooperative Commonwealth Youth Movement."[2]

With the assistance of the Party the Y.C.L. approached youth organizations in all parts of the country with a view to united youth action. A joint youth council sprang up in Winnipeg and was followed by others in various parts of the country. On May 23-25, 1936, the National Youth Congress was founded at a national conference at Ottawa.

The reader needs but to cast his mind back to the

conditions described a few pages earlier, which culminated in the great trek of the camp workers to Regina, and remember that preparations for that trek had already started when the Youth Congress was founded, to realize how intensely young Canadians felt the need for action to save their generation. It should not be assumed that only the revolutionary youth felt this need. The Youth Congress movement included in its ranks official representatives of the youth organizations of the United Church, the Anglican Church and the Catholic Church. Perhaps the best example of how political discussion was raging in non-labor youth organizations is to be seen in the type of resolution submitted to the foundation conference by the delegates from the Young Men's Bible Class of the Riverdale United Church in Toronto. The delegate who submitted the resolution explained that it had been discussed and amended by the membership of the Bible Class over a period of three months to ensure that it expressed their considered opinion. It was a document of nineteen paragraphs, entitled "Canadian Youth and World Peace." The first paragraph stated the general attitude of the members of the Bible Class in the following words:

"We are convinced that there can be no definite peace policy for Canada under the existing system that produces for profit, because we are convinced that the profit system is tied up with, and integrated with war, and that war is an inevitable result of the profit system."

The following paragraph of the resolution was a call to the youth to unite for action. It read:

"We are determined that we shall cooperate to the fullest extent possible with any group whatsoever at attempts to reorganize the existing order for peace, social justice, and economic equality, regardless of their political, social, religious or racial affiliation."[3]

The National Committee of the Communist Party greeted such expressions of the will to unity with gratification. The

128

committee declared:

> "We Communists welcome this statement sincerely. One of our tasks is to seek that possible common ground upon which we, as revolutionary materialists, can join with members of the church who see the evils of the present system and want a better life, in the struggle for peace and a new social order."[4]

To an increasing extent, the work of the Y.C.L. became that of furthering and enriching the united front activities of the Youth Congress movement and its local youth councils. The Y.C.L. played a leading role in the fight for the Youth Bill: prepared by the Youth Congress, submitted to the cabinet and made a subject of public discussion by committing members of parliament to support of it. As the menace of war became increasingly acute, the fight to mobilize the youth of Canada for peace took front rank along with the fight for the Youth Bill, economic protection of the youth and repeal of the Military Service Act. Along with the Communist Party, the Youth Congress movement became one of the fighters for a policy of national reconstruction. As its national secretary pointed out in his booklet, *Canada's Youth Comes of Age*:

> "Four or five years ago, it could have been said with truth that youth, by and large, was apathetic. The force of the depression had not served at that time to stimulate youth to action. Young men and women still lived and acted in the pre-depression ways: enjoyed sports, dances, movies, etc.; and were not interested in 'serious' questions like economics, and social and political issues. As more and more left school or graduated from colleges and there was no work and no immediate prospect of security, youth began to waken up. There was a hardening that was healthy. Pessimism is giving way to calmer, more deliberate study of the situation and planning of action. Youth is becoming serious-minded as it faces more frankly and honestly the world in which it has to live, *the*

world it has to change. Youth is realizing that its own future is at stake. Youth is assuming responsibility for decision and action. Quickly youth is training for citizenship and administration. Perspective is being regained. The certainty of our natural wealth and the calibre of our people are great encouragement for young Canadians; the pioneer past is remembered; the future is for us to build."[5]

Note

1. Stalin's characterization.

2. *Reports and Resolutions*, Ninth Plenum C. P. of C., p. 98.

3. Quoted in *Report of Tenth Plenum*, C. P. of C., 1936, p. 42.

4. *Report of Tenth Plenum*, C. P. of C., 1936, pl; 16.

5. *Canada's Youth Comes of Age*, Kenneth Woodsworth, p. 16.

CHAPTER TEN: A People's National Program

THE EIGHTH national convention of the Communist Party of Canada was held October 8-13, 1937, in the Masonic Temple, Toronto. The convention celebrated the centennial of the struggle for Canadian independence; paying a solemn tribute to the rebels of 1837 and dedicating the Communist Party to continue the historical struggle. Declaring proudly "We are the heirs of '37," the convention emphasized also the tremendous changes that had taken place during the 100 years that had passed:

> "The Canada that Mackenzie and Papineau sought to free was scarcely more than a group of isolated semi-feudal colonies, lacking effective contact with each other and communication with the world at large. Canada, today, is a highly industrialized country with a standard of technical development equal to any in the world."[1]

That was a bare statement of fact, then becoming evident to millions of Canadians. The constitutional provisions of the British North America Act, enacted in 1867, were in glaring conflict with the highly concentrated monopoly-capitalist economy of Canada in 1937. In illuminating contrast to the lack of effective communication with each other and the world at large that had characterized the colonies in 1837, finance capitalism had by 1937 concentrated control of the nation's production and commerce in the hands of a tightly knit oligarchy and had involved Canada deeply in the imperialist struggle for redivision of the capitalist world market. The convention opened with a ceremonial session at the Mutual Street Arena, in which more than 4,000 workers participated in an inspiring tribute to the 1,280 young Canadians who were in Spain in the ranks of the

Mackenzie-Papineau Battalion fighting against fascism.

History had moved through a full cycle since 1837. The cycle was illustrated by the contrast between the contents and proposals of the convention report and the history of the revolutionary struggle of 1837 which was published as part of the Party's celebration of the centenary. A paragraph in that book illustrated the contrast between class relationships as they were in Canada in 1837 and the class relationships prevailing at the time of the eighth national convention.

> "Responsible government, the main demand of the Canadian reform movement, was primarily a means to an end: the breaking of colonial and feudal fetters to allow the economic expansion of an industrial Canada. In this, the aims of the manufacturing class coincided with the general interests of the mass of the people; the industrial bourgeoisie played the role of a revolutionary-democratic force."[2]

The handful of individual land-grabbing office-holders who constituted the "Family Compact" of 1837 had been replaced by a highly organized finance-capitalist oligarchy. Through the systematic interlocking of boards of directors, that oligarchy controlled the vast and intricate machinery of finance, production, transportation, communication and, through its chosen political representatives, the state. Even the ambitions which motivated the modern oligarchy in gradually asserting their freedom from British domination was not an ambition for the independent, industrial development of Canada. It was so that they could sell Canada to United States imperialism. In 1937 monopoly-capitalism already was becoming less interested in the all-round development of Canadian economy and increasingly interested in the quick profits to be made by selling Canada's irreplacable natural resources and territorial independence to the United States.

The eighth national convention drew the attention of all

132

Canada to that profound contradiction between the interests of the overwhelming majority of the people, the real nation, and the so-called "national aims" of monopoly-capitalism. The convention called upon the workers and farmers of Canada to recognize that the real interests of the nation are the interests of the masses of its people. The thesis around which all its resolutions were built was that Canadians were confronted by the necessity for decision-the real interests of the nation could be served only by the political defeat of the monopolists and the replacement of profits and war by people's welfare in peace, as the sole objective of national policy. It pointed out:

> "The people seek progress, the big financial interests seek to turn the wheel of industry back. The people are democratic, the big financial interests are afraid of democracy. The people want peace, the policies of finance-capital are leading Canada in company with the reactionary powers of Europe towards an imperialist war against democracy and progress. Every man and woman in Canada must take a stand upon these issues."[3]

The situation was a challenge to true Canadians. After seven years of crisis and depression profits were up again above the peak of 1929 while wages remained very close to the lowest levels to which they had been slashed during the crisis. The burden of debt and taxation upon farmers and urban middle-class people bad increased tremendously, their incomes remained at depression levels. Preparations for war had become the keynote of imperialist policy. Reaction was on the offensive. Big financial interests and leading politicians of the two old parties were exploring the possibilities for a coalition of all reactionary parties under the high-sounding title of "The United Canada Association." Fascist organizations, typified by Adrien Arcand's organization in Quebec, were being generously financed by big business in various parts of the country. Men who were recognized as enemies of the people, such as Meighen the father of Section 98, Sir Edward Beatty the advocate of railroad amalgamation, Sir Herbert Holt whose financial operations had led to the ruin of thousands of small-business people, Colonel George Drew the pro-fascist admirer of the Mussolini and Hitler regimes, were advocating a "national government." Later the owner of the Toronto *Globe and Mail* sought to establish an over-all general staff for capitalist reaction under the title of "The Leadership League."

The drive of reaction was motivated by fear of the rising militancy of the workers and farmers as well as by the general turn of imperialism towards policies of fascist reaction and war. The need of the people, the development which could guarantee democratic progress, was "Unity in Action." The convention emphasized in its call to the workers and farmers: ". . . Life itself is opening up splendid possibilities ... united action does not necessarily require unity in one organization; it involves only cooperation to secure certain specific objectives." As part of the party's contribution towards a programmatic basis for such unity, the convention called upon all democratic Canadians to elaborate through joint discussions a people's program built around the following six main heads.[4]

> a) *Legislate for Social Security*
> "The people of Canada want progressive legislation. Canada at the present time has the least progressive social legislation of any except four of the twenty-five countries of the Americas. It is a shameful thing that there still remain three provinces, including wealthy Quebec, which have no Widowed Mothers' Allowance and that, in those provinces which have such legislation, a widow with two children should have to live on less than the inadequate minimum wage prescribed for a single girl. We need unemployment and health insurance legislation which will guarantee, to all victims of sickness or involuntary unemployment adequate maintenance for themselves and their families. Old age pensions at sixty, prohibition of juvenile labor, minimum wages for young male workers,

limitation of hours of labor, are all essential for the protection of the Canadian working people. A central need today is trade union legislation which will guarantee to working people the right to join the union of their own choice and the right to bargain collectively through their own freely chosen representatives."

b)   *Save   Canadian   Agriculture*
"...Canada needs a comprehensive national farm policy. Farmers must be protected against the conditions created by the fact that they sell their products in a market controlled by the buyers and are compelled to buy everything they need in a market controlled by the sellers..."

c)   *A   Democratic   Fiscal   Policy*
"The fiscal policy of the Dominion and the provinces needs a complete revamping ... the tax structure needs to be drastically reorganized. ... The nation's currency and credit should be under the control of a nationalized banking system."

d)   *Give   Our   Youth   a   Chance*
"The National Youth Commission established by the King government marks the beginning of governmental recognition of the fact that the problems of the youth of Canada have become a matter of national concern. ... The beginning made is totally inadequate but it shows that the Youth Bill and other proposals advanced by the Youth Congress are practical and should be given effect."

e)   *A   Democratic   Constitution   for   Canada*
"... The Communist Party proposes that the labor and progressive movement of Canada should cooperate through legislative conferences in the formulation of proposals towards the working out of a democratic constitution for our country and join forces in the effort to secure its adoption. Provincial rights must be fully

protected. The constitution of Canada must guarantee complete provincial autonomy and control in all matters concerning civil liberties, education, cultural and religious rights and in all matters concerning the organization and coordination of municipal and provincial governments. ... Appeals to the Privy Council must be abolished. Canada's parliament must be competent to decide."

f) *A Foreign Policy That Makes for Peace*
"... We object to Canada being gradually and insidiously involved in the diplomatic entanglements which are the 'spiders' webs' of the schemers who are working out the plans for a new balance of power and imperialist war in Europe. ... Never before has there been such a widespread and general desire among the people for peace. ... But it is not enough to merely condemn war, we must influence government policy upon issues which are concrete and urgent today. This requires mighty mass movements in support of peace. ... As Mr. Peter Bryce, Moderator of the United Church, has said: 'The mighty power of sentiment against all that is involved in modern warfare may yet save the world from disaster if it is expressed, individually and collectively by the people of the world, and if it is crystallized into action by governments, compelled to do so through the sheer force of the weight of public. opinion.'...

"... We must organize tens of thousands of people in all the constituencies of Canada to bring pressure to bear upon their members of parliament, to demand of them that they place themselves on public record against war. Every candidate for public office should be asked for a similar pledge. Peace-loving people must be aroused to the fact that the issue of peace or war is being decided now. Continued retreat before the fascist offensive means war. If we want peace we must defend it."

In addition to the draft program of which these quoted

sections are typical, the convention adopted resolutions setting forth specific demands for the youth, for the women, for the farmers, for the native Indians, for French Canada; for a foreign policy based upon Canada's interests, etc. The following excerpts are typical.

"Being deeply concerned with the welfare of Canada's youth, the party must focus its attention on their outstanding needs and generate mass movements for their immediate realization, making the struggle for the needs of the youth an integral part of all economic and political struggles of the working class. Our party must offer practical programs for legislation on behalf of the social and economic needs of youth and champion their enactment. ... Such legislation should include: minimum wage laws and stipulations for their enforcement; establishment and extension of vocational and technical training; introduction of a system of apprenticeship under trade union supervision; adequate scholarships for needy students; grants to farm youth; creation of recreational youth centres, etc."[5]

"This eighth convention of our party places before our whole membership and all party bodies the immediate task of carrying on an intensive educational campaign within the party and the labor movement for the correct appraisal of work amongst women. Our leading party bodies still seriously underestimate this vital work and consider it in the main to be the work of women themselves rather than the work of the whole party. Our party has not yet fully grasped that the organization of women requires particular attention to their special problems and needs; hence special forms of organization for which capable trained leadership must be provided. Opinions are still encountered in our party minimizing the importance of organization of women, opposing special efforts in this regard, critical of special women's

137

organizations, disdainful of the contribution which women can make to the labor movement. Such views have hindered the recruiting of women into the party and have led to a tendency on the part of many women comrades to be unwilling to devote themselves to organization of women, since this is falsely regarded as less important than other fields of party work."[6]

Limitations of space prevent reproduction of the entire text of the programmatic proposals put forward by the eighth national convention, as they do of numerous other important documents. The key passages quoted above do illustrate, however, the fundamental fact emphasized by that convention, that the workers are now the only class whose interests as a class are completely identical with the true interests of the nation.

Comparison of the draft People's Program adopted by the eighth convention with subsequent developments shows that, while only a few of the reforms advocated there have been achieved, the formulation of specific and well-defined immediate, political objectives is, in itself, a vital contribution to the popular struggle for democracy and progress. Most of the legislation advocated in that draft is now recognized as necessary by the majority of Canadians.

Note

1. *Monopoly vs. the People*, by Tim Buck. p. 6.

2. *1837: The Birth of Canadian Democracy*, Stanley Ryerson, Francis White Publishers, Toronto, p. 47.

3. *Monopoly vs. the People*, p. 8.

4. *Monopoly vs. the People*, pp. 25-29. Limitations of space prevent reproduction of the entire text of the draft program but the sentences quoted are typical.

5. *Resolutions of the Eighth Dominion Convention*, C. P. of C., p. 51.

6. *Resolutions of the Eighth Dominion Convention*, C. P. of C., p. 58.

CHAPTER ELEVEN: The Communist Party In the Constitutional Crisis

THE EFFECTS OF THE CRISIS emphasized the need for a thorough-going change in the responsibilities of the various levels of government in Canada. The facts of highly concentrated monopoly-capitalism in 1938 contradicted the assumptions upon which the British North America Act was based in 1867. One of the last acts of R. B. Bennett, as prime minister, had been to enact a series of bills termed collectively "Bennett's New Deal." This "death-bed repentance" legislation provided for the establishment of national unemployment insurance, the eight-hour day and other overdue reforms. One of the first acts of Mackenzie King when he became prime minister again was to refer Bennett's "New Deal" legislation to the Supreme Court of Canada. The public reason given was "to test its validity." The actual reason -was to get rid of it without Mackenzie King, the reformer, having to shoulder the opprobrium of repealing reform legislation. Chief counsel for the federal government in that case was none other than Mr. Louis St. Laurent, K.C.

The Supreme Court disposed of the "New Deal" and, so far as legislation was concerned, the workers and farmers of Canada were back where they started from. They were not "back where they started from" politically, however. Disintegration of the two old parties of Canadian capitalism had started and King's action speeded up the disillusionment of tens of thousands who had previously supported, the Liberal Party. Broad sections of the population were groping for progress. The vote cast in the federal elections had given victory to the Liberals but, politically, it was a vote against the Conservative Party and the policies that it stood for.

Mackenzie King never favored thoroughgoing reform of

the constitution, he never advocated any basic change in the division of governmental responsibility provided for in the British North America Act. But a great many municipalities were broke. Those that were not broke were unable to provide even the minimum of relief needed. Several provincial governments were in similar straits. Despite some improvement in the general economic situation there was no improvement, in the conditions of the masses of the people. At the height of the so-called "economic recovery," 925,000 Canadians were still on relief. The crisis in agriculture persisted throughout the "recovery period." After the farmers of the western provinces succeeded in getting a price of 80 cents per bushel set for the 1938 wheat crop, the Dominion government attempted to get it reduced again to 60 cents for the 1939 crop. Eventually a compromise price of 70 cents per bushel was reached.

Canadians were beginning to learn by their own experience that the workers are the only class whose interests as a class are completely identical with the true interests of the nation. As the Communist Party pointed out:

> "The essence of the conflict over the minimum price guarantee of wheat is no less than the question of whether or not Canada can afford to allow western agriculture to decay. Every consideration of national welfare shouts *no!* . . . Our national economy can't operate without production of Prairie wheat, but if western Canada is to remain a wheat producing area there must be a guaranteed price sufficient to enable the farmer to live.... The reason a guaranteed price level is necessary for wheat is to be found in governmental policies which maintain a high price level for everything the farmers buy. . . .
> "The time has now arrived when monopoly-capital is taking such a large percentage of the national income in rent, interest and profits, that a redistribution of income is absolutely essential if the people are to live . . . I submit to you that this problem must be dealt with as a *national*

emergency on a *national* scale. The people of eastern Canada cannot improve their lot unless yours improves also, and vice-versa."[1]

That statement did but emphasize a fact that was acknowledged, tacitly, by Mackenzie King when he appointed the "Royal Commission on Dominion-Provincial Relations." The royal commission was Mackenzie King's roundabout method of "reporting progress" while postponing action to solve the problems of the millions of Canadians who were victims of the crisis and the depression.

Let there be no mistake, the Royal Commission on Dominion-Provincial Relations was of tremendous importance. It received briefs from hundreds of organizations and associations as well as from provincial governments in public hearings. At tremendous cost to Canadian taxpayers the commission produced voluminous studies and a comprehensive report. Its three volumes of summarized findings and proposals did offer Canadian capitalism a mildly liberal program of constitutional reform. The fact that the monopolists rejected that program, preferring to maintain the present constitutional barriers to social reform, emphasizes the arrogance of their reaction. It is probably true that Mackenzie King knew in advance that the monopolists would not accept those proposals but, in his King-esque way, he established a political landmark by securing that plan for social and constitutional changes as the reform alternative to the reactionary program of monopoly-capital.

The only political party which submitted a brief to the royal commission setting forth a documented analysis of the source of the crisis and a full program of constitutional reform, was the Communist Party of Canada. That significant fact mirrored one of the peculiarities in the national life of our country; namely, the contradiction between the material conditions of monopoly capitalism which had rendered the problem of Dominion-provincial relations acute, and the relative political backwardness that the capitalists and their political

142

representatives had been able to maintain. Here was a royal commission set up to study the central constitutional problem of Canadian capitalism. The problem was acute. Any legislation that might result from the work of the commission would have a profound effect for good or ill upon the masses of Canadians - its work was bound to affect their national future. The problem before the commission could be dealt with to the advantage of the masses of the people only by changes to which the monopolists were opposed openly and bitterly. None of the other political parties was prepared to join in a genuine struggle against monopoly-capital, so they ducked the issue. It is an illuminating commentary upon the level of democratic political action at that time that, except among very limited circles of the C.C.F., there was no protest against. that crass betrayal of democratic responsibility by party leaderships.

The Communist brief was acknowledged by many authorities to be the most comprehensive and fully documented of all those submitted by voluntary organizations. That is important today because modified versions of several ideas put forward in it emerged as features of the proposals eventually submitted by the royal commission.

The point of departure of the party's brief, and the conclusion around which it was built, was stated in its Introduction. Rejecting the misleading interpretations of constitutional history that were then rampant, the brief declared: "The constitutional history of Canada is really the history of the struggle between the democratic masses of workers and farmers and the vested interests and monopolists.... The constitution, insofar as we have a constitution, records some of the formal rights of citizens; but no regard is given to the conditions for exercising those rights. . . . The material basis of real political equality and democracy is lacking because the exploiting class dominates the economic life of the nation. The masses have attained democratic rights through their struggles for economic improvement and security against the vested interests.

143

Constitutional principles must therefore be understood in reference to this struggle of the people."[2]

Governmental admission of the necessity for the royal commission had been compelled by the extreme poverty of the many in contrast to the fabulous riches of the few. By government statistics the Communist Party's brief proved that the concentration of wealth and economic power had brought about a situation in Canada in which a numerically small group of monopolists bad been able to maintain their corporate and personal incomes at the expense of the masses of the people, even in the year 1934 when the national income as a whole was down to only 60 percent of the 1929 level. The brief showed that in 1934, the last year for which official statistics were then available, the national income produced by Canadian workers was divided as follows:

Dollar worth of the national income produced	$3,600,000,000
Income from foreign investments	100,000,000
Wages and salaries (including salaries of directors, bank and railroad managers, etc.)	1,840,000,000 (50%)
Farmers' income	440,000,000 (12%)
Employers and workers on their own account	300,000,000 (8%)
Income on investment (rents, interest, profits)	1,130,000,000 (30%)

As those figures show, the investment interests who owned Canada's banks and industries and exploited Canada's natural resources (exclusive of the farms) made $1,130,000,000 just through the fact of ownership. By simply owning and controlling the decisive sectors of Canadian economy, they received 30 per cent of all the values produced that year.

The brief showed further that only 23,600 Canadians, only one fifth of one per cent of the population, had incomes of more than $5,000 during that year. But that one fifth of one per cent of the population received $940,000,000, half as much as was received by all the millions of workers whose labor had produced the national income. Concerning this fact, the brief showed how the income tax laws are framed so as to tax only a small part of the income that the rich make. Describing the technique by which the income tax laws tax the rich only for what the government calls their "taxable net income," it showed that:

> "It is possible for a Canadian millionaire to increase his fortune from 1 to 100 millions without paying a penny of personal income tax on the 99 millions he has made. Profits made but re-invested without ever taking the form of dividends are not profits in the eyes of the law. Under such laws the 'taxable income' of the rich is really only their living expenses, and this, coupled with evasion, means that only one dollar in every three that the rich make in a year is declared and taxed. Our capitalist class makes in a bad year $500 to $600 millions beyond, what it pays income tax on. Yet when pittances are asked of governments to keep hundreds of thousands from starving to death, the capitalists coolly ask 'Where is the money going to come from?' "

Then, as now, the opponents of a thoroughgoing democratic re-shaping of the constitution to bring it into line with modern conditions were concerned only to maintain the British North America Act as a barrier against needed reforms. The Communist brief challenged that attitude and put forward a comprehensive program of reforms indicated in the following summary.

"National Measures Required to Meet the Needs of the

"The Communist Party of Canada proposes that responsibility for all social legislation shall be assumed by the Dominion government. Specifically, we ask that the Dominion government become fully responsible for:
1) Unemployment Insurance and Relief.
2) Health Insurance.
3) Crop Insurance.
4) Minimum National Standards of Education.
5) Housing.
6) Mothers' Allowances.
7) Old Age Pensions.
8) Aid to Youth.

"In addition, we propose that the Dominion government shall assume control of all legislation relating to labor and take steps to institute:
1) Maximum Hours for Labor.
2) National Minimum Wages for Women and Young Workers.
3) National Standards of Minimum Working Conditions.
4) Enforcement of the Right of Workers to Organize in Trade Unions.

"Lastly, there are two other matters which should be transferred entirely to the Dominion, so that much needed action can be taken. The first is control of all companies to the end that the Dominion shall be able to control the monopolies which at present act as complete dictators of the economic life of the country. The second is that the Dominion government shall be given the necessary powers to establish minimum prices for agricultural products."[3]

As noted above, the report of the commission, submitted

by Mr. Justice Sirois[4] included modified versions of several of the proposals put forward in the Communist Party's brief. The report was rejected by Premiers Hepburn of Ontario and Duplessis of Quebec, with the active support of Pattullo, premier of British Columbia. They broke up the Dominion-Provincial Conference convened to consider implementation of the report.

With a sigh of relief that was almost audible, the King government shelved the report. In agreement with the provincial premiers, Mackenzie King introduced substitute makeshift measures which enabled the federal government to raise revenues to cover expenditures that were approved of by the finance-capitalist interests, without committing it to the social reforms recommended by the Rowell-Sirois royal commission.

The fact that the federal government has been compelled to introduce other substitute measures to deal in some measure with the problems of unemployment insurance, contributory old age pensions, and to amend the constitution in conformity with its immediate needs in each case, does not in any way justify the criminal manner in which the elaborate findings of the Rowell-Sirois commission were shelved - without even a pretence at serious study. That was an act for which Canadians will some day condemn the Liberal Party. The changes that the Liberal government has made in the B.N.A. Act, while refusing to consider the establishment of a democratic method by which the Canadian people can amend their constitution, all confirm the fact that the program put forward by the Communist Party to solve the constitutional crisis expressed the urgent democratic needs of the Canadian people.

Note

1. "The West and the Federal Elections," radio broadcast by Tim Buck, Winnipeg, 1938. Sentences excluded from the broadcast by

CBC censorship were retained in the published text.

2. *Submission of the Dominion Committee of the Communist Party of Canada* to the Royal Commission on Dominion-Provincial Relations, 1938. pp. 6-7.

3. Submission of the Communist Party of Canada, p. 41.

4. The Hon. N. Wesley Rowell, K.C., and Mr. John Dafoe of Winnipeg died before the report was published.

CHAPTER TWELVE: Sabotage of Collective Security

TOWARDS THE END of the 1930's Hitler's drive to a predatory expansionist war became evident to all who did not deliberately refuse to see. At the same time the disarmament proposals and the program of collective security put forward by Maxim Litvinov in the name of the Soviet government won the support of widening circles of peace-loving people. The Soviet disarmament proposal was the democratic and peaceful alternative to the imperialists' plans for war. The Communist Party had campaigned consistently for more active Canadian support for disarmament and the strengthening, of the League of Nations. The eighth national convention restated the position of the party on that issue in a comprehensive resolution on Canada's foreign policy. The convention called upon the government:

> To accept full responsibility in the League of Nations and to exercise full Canadian sovereignty in the field of foreign policy.
> To help strengthen the machinery of the League of Nations' action in accord with its covenant.
> To stop Canadian support of the then British policy of cooperation with Hitler and Mussolini (loans, credits, strengthened diplomatic relationships, etc.).
> To cooperate with all other peace-loving countries on the American continent, uniting the weight of those forces against the drive to war.
> To live up to the letter and spirit of the Kellogg Peace Pact and other international treaties and obligations.
> To remove the ban on the export of arms and materials to the legal democratic Spanish government.
> To give full support to China in its just resistance against Japanese invasion. To stop the shipment of war materials

149

to Japan.

To nationalize the nickel industry and to tax heavily all profits made from war contracts.

Then, as now, the Communist Party with all genuine supporters of peace insisted that way was not inevitable. But the eighth convention reiterated the thesis put forward by Norman Freed in his earlier elaboration of the official party position on foreign policy that, "He who does not fight for peace, cannot avert war."

> "*War if not inevitable.* War can be prevented by the might of the people. We can, by our united struggle, bar the road to the warmakers, we can preserve peace, we can prevent fascism."[1]

The peace policy advocated by the Communist Party could have barred the road to the fascist drive to war had energetic, united, democratic action been developed on a sufficiently broad scale. It was evident, however, that the great international finance-capitalist interests and the governments in their service were looking to the "anti-Comintern axis" to solve the problems of the imperialist system by Hitler's "*drang nach Osten.*"[2] Governments which could have made collective security effective were determined to destroy it. By the Anglo-Italian Treaty the Chamberlain government had in effect, endorsed Mussolini's bloody rape of Ethiopia and his invasion of Spain. Advancing millions of pounds along with the treaty, the British government saved Mussolini from economic disaster and literally underwrote his regime. By granting a "standstill" agreement to Hitler, enabling him to use the proceeds of German exports to Britain to buy British goods without paying for British exports into Germany for the time being, the Chamberlain government helped to finance the German war preparations. As the general secretary of the party pointed out: "Men who have enjoyed power, whose forefathers in many cases enjoyed power, allied with others who represent vested financial interests . . . are straining every nerve to build up Hitler as a barrier against the people who want to achieve a better life and extending democracy."[3]

Hitler seized Austria, then the Sudeten. The imperialist governments who had given their solemn pledge to go to the defence of Austria if she were attacked, refused to take any action. When Czechoslovakia was attacked the Soviet government called upon its partners, Britain and France, to take the action to which they were pledged, but they refused. Instead of acting to maintain the integrity of Czechoslovakia, Neville Chamberlain and Edouard Daladier, premier of France, flew to Germany to meet in a friendly discussion with Hitler and Mussolini. Together they hatched the cynical bloodstained Munich Pact.

Political reactions to the Munich Pact revealed with increasing clarity the sharpening line of division in world politics. Numerous public men who previously had given lip service to the idea of collective security recognized in the Munich Pact an unacknowledged alliance between British and German imperialism. Victims of their own wishful thinking that Hitler would extend his Nazi empire only to the East, they joined the chorus of approval. No serious effort was made to maintain the pretence that the "peace in our time" proclaimed by Chamberlain meant peace for all mankind. There was cynical, tacit admission that Chamberlain's hope was peace for British imperialism; while Hitler destroyed the first workers' state. It is important to note the contrasting reactions of the leaderships of the Communist Party and the C.C.F. The Communist attitude was expressed in the following words written by Tim Buck:

"The only effect it can have is to strengthen Hitler's power for aggression, strengthen the fanatical belief among the Nazis that the great democracies are afraid, provoke widespread breakdown of confidence in international treaties, a far-reaching drift of small states from the orbit of French-British influence toward the Rome-Berlin axis and open the door wide to European war, with Hitler in a much more favorable position."[4]

Every Canadian, indeed every adult in the world who is possessed of even elementary information concerning the events of 1938-39, knows that the above-stated position of the Communists was correct. It has been vindicated completely by history. But what was the position of the leaders of the C.C.F.? The following quotation from a front-page story in the *Calgary Herald* describes the C.C.F. position perfectly:

"NATIONAL LEADER OF C.C.F.
BELIEVES CHAMBERLAIN DID
'ONLY THING HE COULD HAVE'

"'Chamberlain did the only thing he could have', stated J. S. Woodsworth, M.P., federal leader of the C.C.F. Party, when he discussed the recent world crisis and Canada's foreign policy at a meeting of the Knights of the Round Table in the T. Eaton Company's dining room at noon today.
"... Mr. H. S. Patterson, K.C., thanked Mr Woodsworth on behalf of the club 'for his acceptable view of the recent crisis'."[5]

All attempts to achieve collective security having failed, the Soviet government attempted to secure a military alliance, binding itself and the British government to mutual assistance against a Nazi attack upon either one. The Chamberlain government rejected the Soviet proposal for a military alliance. British-Soviet negotiations were broken off and the Soviet government entered into negotiations with the Nazi government. Out of these negotiations came the Soviet-German Non-Aggression Pact. Chamberlain's scheme had ended in fiasco. His government had egged Hitler on to the very threshold of war, gambling that he would make war only against the Soviet Union. The Soviet government had exhausted every possibility of securing agreement with the British government for mutual

152

military assistance to prevent Hitler from launching a world war. The Chamberlain government cynically had prevented such an agreement. But the fascists' aim was world conquest, not to "pull chestnuts out of the fire" for British imperialism. The decisive issue at stake was, in fact, fascist world conquest or military defeat of the fascist powers. Lacking Soviet-British agreement, the Soviet-German Non-Aggression Pact was the sole alternative by which the Soviet government could maintain the conditions for the defeat of Hitler's plan. The Soviet-German pact guaranteed the defeat of the fascists; the Chamberlain government paid the political price of its own reckless adventurism.

Note

1. Norman Freed, Report on A Foreign Policy for World Peace - *A Democratic Front for Canada.* New Era Publishers, Toronto, 1938, p. 109.

2. "Drive to the East."

3. *War in Europe,* Tim Buck, p. 14.

4. *The Daily Clarion,* Toronto. Quoted by Sam Carr in *National Affairs Monthly,* April, 1944, p. 16.

5. *Calgary Herald,* October 11, 1938.

CHAPTER THIRTEEN: Against Imperialist War

ON SEPTEMBER 1, 1939, Hitler invaded Poland. What had appeared until then to be separate acts of aggression by the fascist states were transformed into an open all-out war for world imperialist supremacy.

The cynical and terrible gamble upon which Chamberlain had staked the imperialist interests of Britain had led to a fiasco, as Stalin publicly had warned him it would. On Sunday, September 3rd, the CBC broadcast the news that the British government had declared war. In the course of the same day, Prime Minister King announced over the radio that Canada would stand "shoulder to shoulder" with the mother country.

The leadership of the Communist Party had to estimate the real meaning which lay behind the deceitful governmental pronouncements. It had to decide what was the real character of the war and its aims and what should be the attitude of the class-conscious workers toward it. The answers to those questions were provided by the concrete facts of the situation. As Lenin pointed out concerning the first world imperialist war:

> "From the point of view of Marxism, that is, of modern scientific socialism, the fundamental question for socialists in discussing how this war should be appraised, and what our attitude towards it should be, is the objects of the war and the classes which prepared and directed it. We Marxists are not among those who are opposed to all wars. There are wars and wars. We must examine the historical conditions which give rise to each particular war, the class which conducted it and for what objects. Unless we do this, all our arguments about war will be reduced to futility, to a wordy and barren controversy."[1]

The imperialists made elaborate attempts to maintain a pretence that they were at war with Hitler because they were opposed to aggression. Their pretence was made possible and even plausible to the majority of people by the cunning rapidity with which the British and French, governments had destroyed collective security and negotiated the Munich Pact in the guise of a search for peace. The truth was that the Munich Pact was the imperialists' official repudiation of their previous solemn treaty pledges. In relationship to the aim of collective security under the aegis of the League of Nations, it was the same sort of imperialist double-dealing as is the North Atlantic Treaty Organization today.

Confused temporarily by the superficial appearance of British action against Nazi aggression, the leadership of the party made a false estimate. Against an imagined danger of a "super-Munich," it called for simultaneous support of the war and a political struggle to compel the Chamberlain government to wage a genuine anti-fascist war.[2] The party's call for a 'fight on two fronts" was scarcely published, however, before the facts of the situation showed it to be wrong. It was an imperialist war, between imperialist powers, for imperialist aims on both sides. Millions of "little people" were waging just struggles in defence of their homes against aggression but they did not and could not determine the aims of the war - certainly not the aims of the British and Canadian imperialists.

True, there was confusion among the imperialists. Some of them failed to recognize the fact that the Hitler-Mussolmi-Mikado alliance was out to wrest imperialist supremacy in Europe and Asia front the older imperialist powers. Failing to recognize that, many of them, typified in Canada by Col. George Drew, urged cooperation with Nazi Germany to "rid the world of Russian Communism." The persistence of the basic imperialist aim of cooperation with Hitler for the destruction of the socialist state was the reason for the "phoney war" in Europe. Essential war materials of which the Allies were desperately short were still being shipped to Japan as late as the fall of 1941.

The record shows that not only Col. Drew, but the Chain berlain government and Chamberlain's supporters all over the world, fatuously nursed their dream of a rapprochment betwee I n the British government and Hitler, for joint action against the Soviet Union, right until Dunkirk. Sir Neville Henderson, British ambassador to Germany at the outbreak of the war, described in his book "The Mission that Failed," how lie made a direct personal appeal to Hitler at midnight, August 31st, to recognize that all Gerrriany's ambitions could be fulfilled in cooperation with the British government. Henderson's book shows definitely that lie did not understand that German imperialism was after the resources of the British Empire, not the blessing of the Chamberlain government. In spite of the evident determination of Hitler to defeat and supplant British imperialism, Lord Lloyd, a member of Chamberlain's cabinet, published a book[3] shortly after the outbreak of the war which was no more and no less than a frantic last-minute semi-official appeal to the Nazis for Anglo-German cooperation in the exploitation of Europe. Lord Lloyd's thesis was that there was "no frontier in eastern Europe which need be a cause for conflict between Britain and Germany" if Hitler would but cooperate with the British government. The book was published with a laudatory introduction by the British foreign minister at the very time when Hitler was "taking over" every country in Europe to which the Chamberlain government had "guaranteed" protection.

The extent to which the Chamberlain government and its friends in Canada were blinded by their dream of Nazi-British cooperation against the socialist state, was provided by the actions of that government in connection with the Soviet-Finnish war.

Finland, so strategically placed for an attack upon the Soviet Union, was under the control of avowed supporters of the German Nazi regime. Their relationships with Germany were described by Sumner Wells, former secretary of state of the United States, in the following words:

156

"It is notorious that both before and after that first war between the Soviet Union and Finland . . . many political leaders in Finland were enmeshed in Hitler's net. Officials like President Ryti and Finance Minister Tanner often functioned as if they were hypnotized by Hitler and Ribbentrop."[4]

The Chamberlain government was well aware of the political affinities and relationships of Mannerheim, Ryti, Tanner and Co. Yet, despite the desperate position of the British troops in France, that government was preparing during February, 1940, to take tens of thousands of troops and masses of its already inadequate arms, ammunition and transport out of the line there for use in Finland - objectively on behalf of Hitler. In addition to the mass of evidence which revealed that intention at the time, there has since been published conclusive evidence that arrangements had already been made for a joint British-French force to be moved to the Finnish front across Sweden.

The *New York Herald Tribune* of September 7, 1947, reported:

"The Swedish foreign ministry published documents Thursday purporting to show that if the Russian-Finnish 'winter war' of 1939-40 had continued two more days, France and England would have sent a force of 50,000 men to aid Finland in fighting the Soviet Union. "The papers said Raoul Nordling, Swedish consul-general at Paris, brought to King Gustave a special message on March 2nd, 1940, from Edouard Daladier, then premier of France, stating that the force would be sent to Finland across northern Norway as part of a plan for a general attack on Russia, to be launched March 15."

That was on the eve of Hitler's all-out drive into France. German preparations for that drive were known. But, instead of preparing to stop it, the Chamberlain and Daladier governments were occupied with a last-minute effort to bring about British-

French-Nazi unity against the Soviet Union.

It was clear that the British government and its Canadian partners were not engaging in a people's war. Their aim was to correct Hitler's "mistake" and restore capitalist unity against the socialist state.

Recognizing the concrete facts of the situation, the leadership of the party quickly corrected its first erroneous position of "a fight on two fronts" and called upon the Canadian people to: "Keep Canada Out of the War!"

More than forty workers were arrested and imprisoned in different parts of Canada for distributing the party's manifesto against war. The Toronto *Daily Clarion* was suppressed, its business manager, Douglas Stewart, was imprisoned for two years because that paper had printed the manifesto of the Communist International on the war. *Clarté*, the only militant French language paper in Canada, was also banned. Frank Towers, an ex-serviceman in Oshawa, Ontario, was sentenced to three months' imprisonment for having sold the *Clarion* before it was banned. In town after town the distribution of handbills was forbidden and trade union organizational campaigns were stopped by the police. Electrical workers in Brockville, Ontario, were informed by the department of labor that their strike for higher wages and a union agreement was illegal because the company was also producing war materials. Scores of similar examples could be quoted. The reiorn of terror was on.

On January 11, 1940, new sections were added to the Defence of Canada Regulations, making, it legal for the authorities to detain a person in custody without trial. The regulations provided also that a person who had committed no offence whatsoever could be arrested and detained *in anticipation of an offence about to be committed.*

By suppression of its press, prohibition of its propaganda and, later, outlawry of its organizations and internment of those of its spokesmen that the R.C.M.P. was able to capture, the government strove to stamp out the influence of the party in the ranks of the working class. It failed, as events were to show. Despite repression and the systematic cultivation of chauvinism and war fever, the party continued to lead large sections of the workers.

The effectiveness of the party's work was reduced, however, by the re-emergenece of erroneous theories concerning the status of Canada, the role of the Canadian bourgeoisie and the extent to which they were responsible for Canada's involvement in the war. Those erroneous theories diverted the attention of the leadership away from the actual tasks that the party should have taken up. They turned the party's membership towards delusions of bourgeois cooperation with the working class in a struggle to complete "the uncompleted bourgeois-democratic revolution." They caused underestimation of the economic struggles of the workers in imperialist war conditions, underestimation of the role of the trade union movement and, therefore, a weakening of efforts to organize the unorganized.

In its attitude towards the imperialist war, however, and the criminal aims of the imperialists, the party never wavered. From the national leadership to the newest member, the party was united firmly in unflinching and uncompromising opposition to the imperialist war. Headed by the party, class-conscious workers waged a heroic struggle. Mrs. Dorise Nielsen, MP, who had been elected in the federal elections of March, 1940, typified their aims while giving voice to their demands. Utilizing the advantages which accrued to a member of parliament, Dorise Nielsen travelled up and down the length and breadth of Canada addressing huge meetings in support of the demand for peace by negotiation and the right of Canadians to advocate it. Her inspired slogan "Democracy Must Live!" became the expression of all that was best in the working-class movement and its fight to take Canada out of the war.

Note

1. Lenin: *The War and the Working Class,* 1917.

2. *The Daily Clarion,* Sept. 8, 1939.

3. *The British Case* by Lord Lloyd, with an introduction by Lord Halifax, His Majesty's Minister for Foreign Affairs.

4. Quoted in *National Affairs Monthly,* April, 1944, p. 16

CHAPTER FOURTEEN: "A National Front For Victory"

THE Nazi invasion of the Soviet Union on June 22, 1941, and the change in relationships that accompanied it, changed the character of the war. As the Communist Party of Canada pointed out:

> ". . . the possible outcomes of the war have been drastically changed. In place of the previous perspectives of peace through joint action of the anti-war forces 1 n the neutral and belligerent countries, or war fought to an imperialist conclusion, the people ... now face the alternative perspectives of: unity of all who are against Hitler's plan of world conquest . . . or complete Nazi victory and a return of the Dark Ages. Such are the fundamental alternatives confronting mankind today."[1]
> "As Stalin declared in his historic call to action of the Soviet people on July 3rd: 'This war with fascist Germany cannot be considered an ordinary war . . . The aim of this national war in defence of our country is not only elimination of the danger hanging over our country, but also aid to all European peoples groaning under the yoke of German fascism . . . Our war for the freedom of our country will merge with the struggle of the peoples of Europe and America for their independence, for democratic liberties. It will be a united front of peoples standing for freedom and against enslavement and threats of enslavement by Hitler's fascist armies'."[2]

Almost a year later the prime minister, Mr. Mackenzie King, admitted that the character of the war had been changed. Addressing the House of Commons on June 10, 1942, he said: "I do not propose to go, at this time, into the reasons which have

161

since occasioned a change of attitude on the part of some. I readily admit that it may have been due in part to the changed character and world-wide scope of the war."

There was complete accord within the Political Bureau of the party that the character of the war had been transformed, but there were differences concerning the manner in which the party should help to ensure a people's victory. Leading comrades who recognized the fundamental transformation in the character of the war failed to see that, precisely because the new alignment of forces was that of the socialist state and the capitalist democracies in a grand alliance against the world alliance of fascist states, the war would change the world. As that decisive fact was recognized party unanimity developed behind the slogan "A National Front for Victory!"

The program of action to arouse and unite the party in the struggle for labor unity for victory, was issued with the party's new slogan as a title. Because of the differences mentioned earlier, the pamphlet bore the following significant warning: "The report printed herein was adopted by the Political Bureau of the Communist Party of Canada on August 28, 1941. It is the official statement of the party's estimation of the war and the tasks it brings forward, and the policy to be followed by the party in the present period. It replaces and supersedes all materials issued previous to its adoption."

A National Front for Victory was a call to the party for a complete reversal of its previous position. It urged the party membership to strain every nerve in the fight for labor unity to win the war. The party did not ask for organizational agreements or party alliances. It used the term "National Front" to express unity of aim and purpose on the part of all Canada's people who stood for the defeat of fascism. "Such a front, cutting across the lines of class and party interests ... will not even necessitate formal political agreements or pacts."

The party emphasized that the change in the character of

162

the war had brought about a fundamental change in the possibilities for the labor movement to play a leading role, even perhaps to win the leadership of the nation. It called upon the labor movement and particularly the C.C.F. to join hands:

"Despite the profound differences between the Communist Party and the leadership of the C.C.F. on questions of socialist philosophy and the strategy and tactics of the class struggle, a united front of our organizations in the effort to destroy Hitlerism is possible. It is not only possible, but vitally necessary. The fundamental interests of the Canadian working-class movement and the Canadian people demand that such a united front be formed now. We urge the broadest unity throughout the country, of C.C.F. and Communist Party organizations, and all allied forces, around our common aim to defeat Hitler and destroy the menace of fascism."[3]

Condemning the slanderous chauvinistic propaganda of the Tories against the workers of French Canada and, equally, the propaganda of pro-fascist elements in the province of Quebec, the party declared its unwavering confidence in the democratic masses of French Canada and their readiness to fight for a just cause. The party statement, supported and elaborated by pamphlets dealing with the special problems of French Canada, pilloried members of Mackenzie King's cabinet for their big share of responsibility for the attitude of the people of French Canada. Those members of the government, with local politicians and clerics in the province of Quebec, gave systematic support to fascist hopes by defending "the men of Vichy," by praise of fascist corporatism as a political philosophy, by cultivating the lie that the main enemy of Canada was communism and the Soviet Union. The party statement declared that such voices did not represent the masses of the people of French Canada. The people are against tyranny, they are against exploitation, they are for bonafide trade unionism. Even as the party's pamphlet was published, the people of French Canada were demonstrating their sentiments by flocking into the trade unions faster than was the case in any other part of Canada.

The party was still banned and compelled to operate underground. Because it was vital that the membership should be unified around the change of policy, it was decided that, despite the evident difficulties, a national conference must be held. An underground conference was organized and held in Montreal in February, 1942. There, party leaders from every part of the country thrashed out the whole question of the transformation of the character of the war, and the transformation made necessary in the work of the party. The main resolution adopted declared: "The Communist Party of Canada gives its unconditional support to the national war effort and to the alliance of the United Nations. . . . The Communist Party calls upon the people of Canada to build national unity around the country's war effort. ... The changed character of the war which has led to the world alliance of the democratic governments and peoples has also created the conditions for a class alliance embracing all classes in the capitalist democracies united by the common aim of defending their national existence. Such a class alliance is developing in Canada.... In this alliance the working class has a great role to play ... the level of its initiative and strength in the war is the measure of the rise of the subjective force of the people's war against fascism."

While emphasizing the necessity for the working class to win a place for itself in the leadership of the nation, the resolution castigated the Liberal government for its anti-working-class policy of freezing wages at depression levels while the profits of Canadian corporations were soaring to new record high levels. It called upon democratic Canadians to insist upon a hundred per cent excess profits tax and increased taxes on big incomes. It called for equal pay for equal work for women and men. It denounced the King government's penny-pinching policy of maintaining two standards of "cost-of-living bonus," with the

164

lower bonus for those workers who needed it most. At the same time, the resolution called upon all democratic Canadians to support the forthcoming plebiscite on the question of compulsory military service:

> "The Communist Party calls upon the Canadian people to vote *yes* on the plebiscite, and directs every party member and organization to unfold a great campaign around the central slogan: *Make the plebiscite into a mighty demonstration of national unity for total war!*"[4]

One of the questions that confronted the conference was: "How shall the party develop a broad public campaign in support of the plebiscite, while tinder governmental ban?" The delegates answered that question by adopting a plan to set up "Tim Buck Plebiscite Committees" all over Canada under the national slogan of "Vote '*YES*' for Victory!" The first committee was in Toronto with headquarters at 601 Yonge Street, headed by Leith McMurray, chairman; Harry Bell, recording secretary; Pearl Wedro, secretary-treasurer. Within a few weeks Tim Buck Plebiscite Committees were functioning in dozens of centres. By leaflets, newspaper advertisements, recordings of speeches and house-to-house canvassing, the committees carried the campaign for a *Yes* vote into every community. Acknowledging that a great many Canadians who wanted to see Hitler defeated were so dissatisfied with the government that they were advocating a *No* vote as a rebuff to the Liberals, the committees urged Canadians to recognize the historic significance of the plebiscite. The central pamphlet issued by the committees placed the question as follows:

> "The plebiscite is now a factor in Canada's war effort. It can be, and it is our task to make it a positive factor. It will help to make all our people fully war-conscious. It confronts every one of us with the responsibility of taking a definite stand: for or against strengthening the nation's war effort. A national campaign to arouse the people and bring out an overwhelming majority to vote *yes* will be

the biggest step forward that we have yet made in developing that offensive spirit, the spirit of attack, which is essential to victory."[5]

The party was banned, none of its prominent leaders was able to participate publicly in the campaign. Tories, as well as avowed pro-fascists, exploited the illegal status of the party to reduce popular support for the campaign but the Tim Buck committees made a powerful impression upon public opinion. The *Montreal Gazette* was impelled to admit editorially after the plebiscite that the only genuine national campaign in support of a *Yes* vote was the systematic and effective campaign carried through by the illegal Communist Party.

To study the lessons of the plebiscite campaign and to maintain the organization that had been built up in the fight for a *Yes* vote, a national conference of representatives of all the plebiscite committees was held in Toronto May 30-31, 1942. The delegates gathered there decided to unite their committees in a nationwide organization of "Communist-Labor Total War Committees." Lieut. William Kardash, member of the Manitoba legislature, was elected national chairman. The Communist-Labor Total War Committees continued the battle for working-class unity to ensure people's victory. They organized conferences of citizens, united groups of workers to fight for the establishment of labor-management committees in the plants. As their campaign developed and support for their program took on mass popular proportions, it became evident that a struggle had to be initiated on a national level to remove the ban from the Communist Party.

It should be pointed out here that the heroism displayed, the magnitude of the battles fought and the crucial significance of the victories being won by the Red Army, were then generating a profound wave of admiration for our Soviet ally. The *Toronto Dally Star*, for example, declared editorially on August 4, 1942: "Russia's strength lies not only in her well-trained army and military leaders. The root of it, a strong root, is in the people from whom the army and its leaders are drawn. The fact is that the entire Russian nation Is literally 'up in arms.' Every household is in this battle, every man, woman and child who is physically fit has a job to do and is doing it."

Great "Salute to Russia" demonstrations were held all across Canada to celebrate the anniversary of the change in the character of the war and of the Soviet-British alliance. Provincial governments, municipal councils, universities, churches, press, etc., paid warm tributes to the Soviet Union and her heroic peoples. There was indeed a flowering of mutual understanding in the democratic and heroic partnership of the war. Even the Toronto *Globe and Mail* was impelled to write editorially on October 15, 1942: "The time for recriminations and the continuance of past prejudices is long past. This newspaper has said some bitter things about the Russians. We have been wrong, and have repudiated many of them."

Meantime, although public enthusiasm for the grand alliance was growing, and the temper of class relationships in Canada increasingly reflected the new, people's character of the war, the Communist Party was still banned. Comrade A. E. Smith, secretary of the National Council for Democratic Rights, launched a campaign to press the government to "Lift the Ban." Communists incarcerated in Internment Camp "H" addressed a collective letter to the prime minister calling upon him to recognize the change that had taken place in Canada's policy as a result of the change in the character of the war, and the advantages that would accrue to the war effort, therefore, by their release. They emphasized that: "Not one of our number has been charged with a single overt act; in not a single case has reason been shown why any should be imprisoned in the interests of the security of the state."

Under pressure of the public appeals the government finally set up a parliamentary committee to study the case.

The minister of justice, Mr. Louis St. Laurent, refused to

consider lifting the ban. There being no I onger any justification for maintaining the ban on the Communist Party because of its attitude toward the war, Mr. St. Laurent resorted to declarations that the fundamental philosophy of the Communists was in conflict with his conception of Christian civilization. It was a striking fact that even in the midst of the war against fascism, Mr. St. Laurent and General Franco used the same terms to excuse their persecution of the Communists. In the name of the Communist Party, its secretary declared: "I would welcome a comparison between our ideals *as expressed in practice* and his own (Mr. St. Laurent's) before any public tribunal in Canada. I have no fear whatever of the outcome"

After lengthy hearings, the parliamentary committee recommended that the ban should be lifted from the Communist Party and the rights of its members to advocate their point of view in public be restored. Still Mr. St. Laurent said no. The committee's report was not submitted to the House of Commons and nothing was done.

In a letter to Mr. St. Laurent, the secretary of the party drew the latter's attention 'to the profound contradiction between his admission that "Canadians belonging to the Communist Party can be helpful in our war effort" and his refusal to implement the committee's recommendation. Tim Buck pointed out that strong personal opinions about the differences between communism and "Christian civilization in our country" did not justify refusal by the minister of justice to implement the report of a parliamentary committee. He continued:

> "To make the fundamental religious or political convictions of a man or a group the test of whether or not they shall be allowed to exercise the full rights of citizenship, as your words do, is to deny the essential principle of democracy ... It is to suggest a return to the principle of the Spanish Inquisition. Your words express an attitude towards Canadians with whose fundamental philosophical convictions you disagree similar to the

attitude of Hitler's most violent adherents towards both the church and anti-fascist activities in Germany."

The party leadership recognized that the difference between whether it could work publicly or be forced to continue underground could make a big difference to the role of Canadian labor in the war effort. This realization was stimulated in July, 1942, by the arrest of Comrades J. B. Salsberg and Joe Gershman. The circumstances were as follows.

As a result of the anti-working-class wage policy of the Liberal government and the manner in which Humphrey Mitchell, minister of labor, enforced it, there was acute danger of a tie-up of the shipyards on the Pacific Coast. Hoping to persuade the workers to refuse to be provoked by, Humphrey Mitchell's arrogance, Joe Salsberg proposed to run the risk of detection and go direct to Vancouver by plane. To secure the agreement of other members of the Political Bureau, he departed from the strict and usually rigid rules of procedure. As a result he was detected by the Mounties and arrested. That touched off a conclusive study by the leadership of the party of the measures necessary to force the issue of party legality.

After a careful canvas of opinions all over the country, it was decided that seventeen of the leading comrades would congregate in Toronto and publicly surrender. On the 10th of September, 1942, the seventeen made their way by various routes to the office of Mr. J. L. Cohen, and announced their intention to the amazed K.C. Then, with what almost amounted to humor, the R.C.M.P., which had failed until then to "get their men," asked the seventeen would 'they "mind coming over to the R.C.M.P. headquarters" at Beverley and Dundas Streets to surrender.

A special tribunal was set up to investigate whether the seventeen, or any of them, should be interned. The tribunal reported *no* upon each case. As the Political Bureau of the party had estimated, release of the seventeen compelled the government to release all the Communists. Within a month they were all free.

Those who were of military age volunteered immediately for overseas service. Several of them were parachuted behind Hitler's lines and served with distinction. A number of Canadian Communists were awarded decorations for service in the field. Some, like Harry Binder who was wounded in action three times, still carry the scars of their service. Some, like Dick Steele, Zane Navis, Muni Ehrlich, Hughie Anderson, Reuben Gorodetsky and others, including several of the comrades who were parachuted behind Hitler's lines, gave their lives in the People's War against fascism.

The leaders of the party, local and national, returned to their homes and took up the battle. In all-sided activity the left-wing movement was mobilized in a campaign of the widest public character to unite labor and win for the working class a leading role in the carrying through of the war effort. Integral with all activities to strengthen labor's role in winning the war, the party took up the fight to compel the King government to change its wage and labor policy. When, under pressure of working-class resentment, Mackenzie King set up a board to hold a national inquiry into wages and labor relationships, the national Communist-Labor Total War Committee submitted a brief which constituted, simultaneously, the wage program of the working-class movement and "A Labor Policy for Total War." Taking as its central idea the thesis that "the battle lines run through the plants of the nation," the brief showed that the inequitable wage and labor policy of the government was, by its rank injustice to the workers, an obstacle to the war effort. The brief castigated the government for its policy which forbade wage increases to 485,526 heads of families whose earnings then averaged only $17.46 per week, while paying so-called "dollar-a-year" men $125 a week for expenses, from which they asked to be excused the obligation of paying personal income tax.[6] It exposed the dishonest makeup of the cost-of-living index. It showed that the real driving forces behind the inflation, then starting were not wages and working-class demands for improved conditions, but the governments systematic expansion of currency and credit while restricting the volume of products coming on the market for civilian consumption - basically the same causes that are operating today. The brief concluded with the following words: "The inquiry your board is conducting is of tremendous importance in the life of our country.... The government will be provided by this inquiry with an opportunity to draw labor into full partnership in the present titanic struggle. We all hope that the government will avail itself of this opportunity."

The party campaigned in every section of the labor movement for support of the all-out war effort advocated in its, brief. Some of the reforms it urged were introduced, albeit cheeseparingly, but the government did not introduce any basic change in its approach to labor. The difficulty of raising these issues to the national level, the fact that the Communist Party was still banned and the. minister of justice was adamant in maintaining the ban, the evidence that it would not be lifted before federal elections were held, and the necessity for a national campaign around a genuine working-class program in the federal general elections, all combined to create an urgent need for "A New Party of Communists."

Note

1. *A National Front for Victory,* p. 3

2. *A National Front for Victory,* p. 7.

3. *A National Front for Victory,* p. 16.

4. *Political Resolution,* National Conference Communist Party of Canada, February, 1942, p. 9.

5. *Vote "YES" on the Plebiscite,* Tim Buck's Appeal, p. 11

6. *A Labor Policy for Victory,* p. 9

CHAPTER FIFTEEN: Again the Issue Of Canada's Status

THE DEMAND FOR establishment of a legal party of Communists was unanswerable. Well-known Communists, could walk the streets again but the party was still banned. Active public work was carried on through the Communist-Labor Total War Committee movement, but there was need for legal political expression on a nation-wide scale of the Communists' liberating ideal of "the People's War." There was need for organized public struggle to achieve a higher role for the working class in the national war effort. Furthermore, there was talk of a war-time election. It was clear that one of the reasons why the government refused to lift the ban was to prevent the Communists from coming before the working class as the party of working-class advance in the struggle for victory. For all these reasons the establishment of a legal party was necessary.

But before founding a new national party it was necessary to deal authoritatively with the erroneous ideas, mentioned in Chapter Thirteen, that had been propagated throughout the party during the period of illegality.

Political differences within the party leadership had revealed themselves in the course of an underground meeting of the full Political Bureau during May, 1940, and had persisted since. The members of the Political Bureau had divided sharply in their estimation of the status and role of Canada and, therefore, on the tasks confronting the working class. The position of the majority   was   summarized   as   follows:
a) The Canadian bourgeois-democratic revolution having been defeated in 1837, the task of completing the "uncompleted" bourgeois-democratic revolution was the decisive task then confronting   the   Canadian   people.

173

b) The Canadian bourgoisie is a dependent bourgeoisie. Canada is caught in the vortex of the Anglo-American conflict one section Of the bourgeoisie being dependent upon and subordinate to British imperialism, the other section being dependent upon and subordinate to United States imperialism.

c) The antagonisms between British and United States imperialism were being aggravated by the war and the conflicting interests of British and United States imperialism were leading to "a crisis of bourgeois rule in Canada."

d) The relationship of the bourgeoisie of French Canada to the bourgeoisie of English-speaking Canada is that of an oppressed bourgeoisie to their oppressors. The political perspective of French Canada is that of national bourgeois-democratic struggle to free French Canada from that oppression. The immediate task of the revolutionary working-class movement in Quebec is to unite the workers in support of the bourgeois-democratic struggle for the fight to national self-determination.

e) Canada's relationship to Britain in 1940 was still a "semicolonial relationship under which Canada has not even nominal control in the basic imperialist question of war and peace."

The manner in which they propagated their theory of the inevitablility of Canada becoming involved in an imperialist war between Britain and the United States is exemplified in the following quotation from an, article which purported to clarify "The dependent relations of the Canadian bourgeoisie and the maturing revolutionary crisis":

> "Only a fool would try to predict when and under what circumstances in relation to other imperialist wars, especially the present one between British and German imperialism, the contradictions between American and British imperialism will break into war. But only a stupid apologist for imperialism, or a social-chauvinist who knows nothing of the real 'economic essence' of imperialism and is sold completely to the service of

174

capitalism can fail to see that the war must inevitably involve U.S. imperialism in war with British imperialism . . ."

On the basis of such arguments the majority proposed that the party's central slogan "Withdraw Canada from the Imperialist War" should be replaced by the slogan "Separation from the Empire."

The minority opposed that position, urging that it tended to turn the face of the party away from its immediate tasks, away from the working class, and away from the direct struggle against the Canadian bourgeoisie. The minority opposed the theory of the "inevitability" of war between Britain and the United States. They argued that: "The immediate effect of the war is to drive British and United States imperialists to subordinate their antagonism and cooperate with each other in defence of their mutual imperialist interests." The minority rejected the theory that a crisis in the ranks of the Canadian bourgeoisie, as a result of sharpening British and American contradictions, was inevitable. They maintained that the basic political contradiction in Canada was between the interests of monopoly-capital and the interests of the masses of the people. They maintained that the political perspective of the working-class movement flowed directly from and was hinged upon that basic contradiction; that the immediate and urgent tasks of the party were to get into and strengthen the numerous wage movements and to unify the struggles of all those sections of the population which, for various reasons, were opposed to increased participation in the war. They insisted that the slogan "Withdraw Canada from the Imperialist War" expressed the unifying motive for broad, popular struggle against the profit-hungry monopolists who were seeking to thrust Canada deeper into the war and into world-wide imperialist entanglements.

Concerning French Canada, the minority maintained that the development of capitalism and of French-English bourgeois relationships had "by-passed" the conditions for bourgeois leadership of the struggle for the national independence of French Canada. The bourgeoisie of French Canada will not lead the struggle for national self-determination. They, along with the upper circles of the hierarchy of the Roman Catholic church in Quebec, are now full partners with the bourgeoisie of English-speaking Canada in exploiting the national market and resources, including the Canadian working class. It is they who maintain the province of Quebec as an area of low wage levels, low standards of education and social services, of exceptionally high capitalist profits. The struggle for the right to national self-determination has yet to be won in French Canada but the bourgeoisie will not lead it; the bourgeoisie has become an enemy of that ideal. Today, only the working class will lead the democratic forces of French Canada to full national self-determination.

So sharp was the split between the members of the Political Bureau that it was impossible to achieve agreement upon policy in the conference at which the differences became evident in May, 1940. The leadership was separated geographically and, as a result, all directives and propaganda material sent out to party organizations throughout the following twelve months were based upon the completely false theory held to by the majority of the members of the Political Bureau. A systematic exposition of the theory was published in a pamphlet entitled *Towards Canadian Independence,* distributed throughout the party in April, 1941.

A plenum was convened, therefore, in January, 1943, attended by nearly 100 leaders of the party. It repudiated the theory of semi-colonialism and the proposals which had flowed out of it. It reaffirmed the position that: "All the essential features of Canada's bourgeois-democratic revolution have been completed, the Canadian bourgeoisie enjoy complete and unquestioned sovereignty." It re-emphasized that Canada's national policies expressed the will of the monopolists. They have the power to modify their state relationships and they exercise that power when it suits their purpose. They did not

176

issue a declaration of independence; on the contrary, they seek still to exploit "the British connection." What those facts reflect "is not lack of Canadian sovereignty but the unity of class interests that has dominated and still dominates the relationships between the British and Canadian imperialist bourgoisie."

The plenum characterized both the general theory that Canada's relationship to Britain was one of semi-colonial subordination and the claim that the struggle confronting French Canada is a bourgeois-democratic struggle, as right-opportunism, reflecting dangerous petty-bourgeois influences within the party. The plenum called upon the party membership to close its ranks around the class policy of national unity for victory over fascism, and to strengthen the working class for the struggles that were bound to follow.

CHAPTER SIXTEEN: A New Party of Communists

ON JUNE 13, 1943, party leaders from all over Canada gathered in conference in Toronto again, this time to plan the establishment of a new party of Communists. Lieut. William Kardash, M.L.A., of Winnipeg, was elected chairman; T, C. Sims of Toronto, secretary. Following a day of intensive discussion, the conference adopted a declaration of purpose[1] of which the following excerpts are characteristic:

> "Humanity has paid a terrible price in, blood and treasure, shattered hopes and human misery, because Hitler was temporarily successful in winning the sympathy of powerful interests in the democratic countries and in duping governments with his fable of the 'Spectre of Communism.'
>
> "Today, no honest man will defend the imperialist appeasement policies of Chamberlain which helped to make Hitler master of Europe. All democratic Canadians applauded Premier King's repudiation of Munich, as Britishers applauded the similar repudiation by the Churchill government.
>
> "History has proven that we Canadian Communists were much closer to reality on these questions than were the editors of the *Toronto Telegram* and *Financial Post*; and that we are far more correct in our fight for the real interests of the Canadian people than were many high-placed personages whose names we forbear to mention here in the interests-of national unity.
>
> "We Communists have fought consistently for democratic unity of French and English-speaking Canada. We have upheld the right of the French-Canadian people to full national equality in all spheres of economic, social and

political life, and first and foremost in labor's struggle on behalf of wage equality for Quebec. We were able to make a notable contribution to the defence of Canadian democracy by our systematic exposure of the treasonable activities of the Nazi-Fascist network operating in Quebec, by our struggle against the Duplessis Padlock Law and our consistent support of the growing democratic trends in French-Canadian life.

"We are not called upon, either by history, the laws of Canada, or the interests of our fellow-Canadians, to renounce our Communist convictions or the proud historic name to which those convictions give us the right. Canadian Communists have fought for those convictions. On the public platform, in city councils, in the trade unions and the factories, in the movements of the unemployed, on the field of battle in defence of democracy in Spain, in the plebiscite campaign, the battle for production, Communists have defended the convictions they hold dear.

"We are Communists. We have a part to play in the winning of the war and the building of Canada. We can play that part fully only if we are free to put forth and fight publicly for our proposals and policies on every question of national concern.

"...this conference constitutes itself a provisional national committee to initiate the work of drawing together the supporters of Communist policies, to prepare a draft program and constitution for their consideration, and to organize a constituent convention to establish such a party of Communists.

"Unite your forces in one powerful Dominion-wide party through which Canadian Communists shall play their full and rightful democratic role in shaping the destiny of this, our wide and rich and lovely land."

The National Constituent Convention convened in Toronto on August 21, for two days of intensive and historic sessions. In an atmosphere of inspired idealism and high enthusiasm 600 delegates established a new national party. From among numerous proposals they chose the name, "Labor-Progressive Party." It should be noted that in periods of illegality the term Labor-Progressive frequently had been the banner of Communist candidates. Shortly before the convention A. A. MacLeod and J. B. Salsberg had been elected in the Ontario provincial constituencies of Bellwoods and St. Andrew, Toronto, as Labor-Progressive candidates, and Fred Rose had been elected in the federal constituency of Cartier, Montreal.

The keynote speech delivered to the convention by Tim Buck[2] reiterated the reasons why immediate organization of the new party bad been undertaken. He pointed out that the majority of Canadians were dissatisfied with the Dominion government's conduct of the War effort, Its evasion of fundamental isues, its systematic favors to powerful corporations that were making unprecedented profits, the steadily increasing burdens upon the working people, its systematic concessions to pro-fascist elements while maintaining a rigid hard-faced attitude towards labor. "We place all our emphasis upon the supreme need to win the war," he declared, but ". . . peace will bring new problems.... It is no wonder that millions of people are asking 'What sort of world shall we build when the fighting stops?' The reply that springs to the lips of every progressive man and woman is 'It must not be the sort of world that we left behind us in 1939'."

At that time, while the British and American governments under the influence of Winston Churchill were delaying the invasion of Europe, it was already evident that hard fighting on the part of the progressive forces would be required to prevent the imperialists from restoring the sort of world that we had known in the 1930's. Tim Buck pointed out that the significance of the grand alliance headed by Britain, the Soviet Union and the United States went much further than military cooperation; it marked *the possibility* of a new era of history. It proved the practicability of intimate collaboration between the first socialist state and the great capitalist states. "Canada will go forward in peace and democracy to a higher life, if the unity of Britain, the United States and the U.S.S.R. is maintained... The alternative is reversion to a world struggle for colonial domination, for trade, for territorial advantage-the old imperialist struggle for power."

Tim Buck warned the delegates that "even while this convention is in progress there are signs which are cause for grave concern." He then quoted numerous examples of sabotage by the capitalist governments, including the Canadian governments, of understandings for co-ordinated action by the members of the grand alliance. Accredited diplomatic representatives of the Soviet government were being excluded from areas under Anglo-U.S. control, the heads of governments in exile were being prevented from leaving Britain to visit the Soviet Union, several of the governments in exile were protesting against the thinly disguised preparations for establishment of Anglo-U.S. military control of their countries after the war. There was indeed serious cause for concern at the signs that the imperialists were planning to scuttle cooperation between the capitalist and. socialist states at the first opportunity. As Charlie Sims was to write immediately after the convention:

> "Powerful forces in Canada and the United States are already working for such disruption. These interests, represented most definitely by powerful investment bankers' associations are bent upon developing a new era of imperialist supremacy and finance-capitalist exploitation.
> "These are the interests which strive to counterpose a British-United States alliance to the Anglo-Soviet-American coalition. Their aim is not that of a lasting peace through collective security and freedom for all peoples, but an imperialist peace in which United States imperialism, with British imperialism as a junior partner,

181

will dominate the world. The more blatant protagonists of this idea openly declare their aim to 'marry the wealth and power of the United States to the territory and resources of the British Empire.'
"If the aims of these interests, which would render impossible the unity of nations visualized in the Atlantic Charter, should become the objectives of foreign policy after the war, the present war will have been fought and won in vain."[3]

The theme of the combined need to strengthen the working-class movement, win higher wages and other concessions from the capitalist class while doing everything possible to ensure victory in the war and to make the war-time unity a force for continued democratic progress in the peace, was carried forward in the party program, which declared unequivocally:

"The Labor-Progressive Party has no interest apart from the general interests of the working class, which are inseparable from the real interests of the nation as a whole. Fighting in the front ranks of the working class at each stage of historical development, the party defends the immediate interests of working men and women and, while so doing, defends their future interests.
"The Labor-Progressive Party is dedicated to the task of educating and organizing the Canadian workers, farmers and middle-class people, in the course of a consistent struggle for democracy, to the end that the majority of the Canadian people shall, by their own decision, achieve the great aim of socialism."

Pointing out that the focal issue in the problem of unity was that of relationships between the two nations, French and English-speaking Canadians, the program declared:

"It is the great movement of labor now arising in Quebec which, in alliance with all other anti-fascist forces, will

182

give increasing political leadership to the anti-trust, anti-imperialist sentiment of the masses of the Quebec people, in the struggle for national unity and people's victory, for full realization of the democratic, national aspirations of the French Canadians."

In this connection the following should be added. The fight to build a mass party of Communists in Quebec, in the face of the Padlock Law, the vicious fascist efforts of the Duplessis government to suppress the labor movement and the anti-working-class obscurantism of the Catholic hierarchy, is a continuing problem, but the rapid growth of trade unionism and the increasing influence of Marxism-Leninism in Quebec, on the background of popular opposition to the underhand cooperation between Duplessis and St. Laurent in selling Quebec into bondage to United States imperialism, show that the workers of French Canada will build their mass Communist party. Already, the contributions of French Canada to the Communist movement have been tremendous. Some of the outstanding contributions to the struggle to organize the unorganized have been made in Quebec. The great needle trades strike, the organization Of the textile, asbestos, electrical, shoe, and other industries, have each provided outstanding examples of working-class militancy. The contributions of French Canada to the development of our party has been tremendous. From those stalwarts among the founders of the Workers' Party, Mike and Beckie Buhay, Bella Hall, Alex Gauld, etc., the party organizations in Quebec have regularly contributed talented and tested members both- to the national leadership and numerous local leaderships of our party. While fighting in the party for more energetic advocacy of the party's demand for the right to full national self-determination to the people of French Canada, the party there has made vital contributions to the building of the Communist movement all over Canada.

Describing the grand alliance as "the harbinger of a world-wide system of collective security in the spirit of the

Atlantic Charter," the program warned the working class that the long-term peaceful co-existence of the socialist states and the democratic capitalist states, expressed in the continued collaboration of the peoples and governments of the U.S.A., Great Britain, the U.S.S.R. and China, was the sole hope of World peace. Emphasizing the dynamic role that the working class would have to play in realizing that objective the program declared:

> "The main task now presenting itself to the Canadian labor movement is to step forward as the champion of the true interests of the people. The movement for independent labor-farmer political action, which is arising in the course of the people's war, must be strengthened and united to carry the war to final and complete victory. The perspective is now before the Canadian labor movement of so consolidating its economic and political strength in cooperation with the farmers, as to elect majorities to the governments of Canada - municipal, provincial, federal - so as to establish labor-farmer governments which can lead the nation in effecting profound democratic reforms in the economy and law of Canada."

The program categorically condemned the lie that the party advocates violence as a means of political struggle. "The Labor-Progressive Party rejects conspiracy and secrecy as political methods and publicly proclaims its program and policy at all times." The program continued:

> "The Labor-Progressive Party categorically denounces force and violence as a means of imposing any form of government or economic system upon the Canadian people. Monopoly, not the labor movement, is the breeder of force and violence. It is the means whereby groups of anti-social, anti-democratic monopolists seek to maintain their power after other means of intimidation and control have failed. It is the means whereby an outworn social

184

system seeks to perpetuate itself."

The basic position of the Communists towards violence expressed in the above quotation, which is so regularly denied or misrepresented by the hired propagandists of capitalism, was emphasized by Lenin during the revolutionary crisis preceding the great Russian Revolution in 1917. Emphasizing the urgent necessity for the working class to take over state power he wrote: "In order to obtain the power of the state, the class-conscious workers must win the majority to their side. As long as no violence is used against the masses, there is no other road to power. We are not Blanquists; We are not in favor of the seizure of power by a minority."[4]

The new party declared itself at its foundation the firmest defender of the real national interests of Canada, the champion of national unity and progress for the Canadian people:

"It seeks to instil in Canadians a deep awareness of the richness of Canada's resources, human and material, and a pride in the great pioneering that remains to be done. It is the champion of the closest fraternity between Canadians of all national origins. It dedicates itself to the flowering of Canadian culture, to the unhampered and state-aided growth of Canadian science, technique, art, literature, culture and education, understanding that the stimulation of all expressions of our national spirit is at the same time a contribution to the cultural wealth of all humanity ...
"For the achievement of these high purposes and the realization of this vision of Canada's destiny, and in the closest unity and brotherhood with all democratic Canadians, the Labor-Progressive Party is established, and hereby calls on all who support the general terms of this program to enrol in its ranks."

The above citations from the program express the fundamental concepts of the founders of the L.P.P. The conviction that, eventually, through their own experiences in which the educating and organizing activities of the L.P.P. will play a vital part, the workers of Canada will, by their own decision, achieve the great aim of socialism. Reinforcing the principles of the program, the constitution and the series of resolutions adopted by the founding convention based the future work of the party unequivocally upon the tested methods of democratic, political education, mass organization and struggle. In the manifesto that the convention addressed to all democratic Canadians, the party introduced itself as follows:

> "We take our part in the mighty labor-farmer movement for independent parliamentary action now springing up as the symbol and instrument of a greater people's wartime democracy, for sweeping national reforms, for a happy post-war Canada and for permanent peace.
> "We call on the trade unions and farm groups to build their organizations and to come forward as part of this rising movement.
> "We can look to a glorious future if the rising labor and democratic movement is united. We look forward to the election of labor-farmer governments which will carry through these great reforms, and which will oppose the monopolies who hinder our country's development.
> "We hail the electoral victories in Ontario, Quebec and the West as the forerunners of such governments.
> "We are a party of socialism. We have undying faith in the ability of Canadians to achieve our true destiny of becoming a mighty industrial nation, affording its citizens the highest living standards in the world, living in harmony with all other peoples and possessed of strong democratic liberties and institutions.
> "The Labor-Progressive Party advocates this platform as its contribution to a better Canada. It will cooperate with all Canadians to achieve these great national reforms and to institute these national policies.
> *"Through unity to victory for progress!"*

Canadian Communists were again a legal political force throughout the nation.

Note

1. *Canada Needs a Party of Communists,* published by the National Initiative Committee to convene a Communist Constituent Convention, June 23, 1943, Toronto.

2. *Victory Through Unity.*

3. *The Keys to Victory,* by Charles Sims, p. 11.

4. Lenin: *Selected Works,* Vol. 6, p. 29.

CHAPTER SEVENTEEN: For a Lasting Peace

PROMPTLY AFTER its founding convention, the Labor-Progressive party launched a great Canada-wide campaign to arouse and mobilize the working-class movement. The need was for united action to win through to the great new possibilities emphasized by the convention and to beat back the threatening dangers against which the convention had warned.

On December 1, 1943, Roosevelt, Churchill, and Stalin, issued their famous joint declaration summarizing the agreements that they had reached at Teheran. From its opening sentence that declaration signalized the opening of a new stage in history. It mirrored recognition by the heads of the decisive imperialist governments of the changed role of the Soviet Union. Under the pressure of the war and the historic military achievements of the Red Army, the political world leaders of imperialism proclaimed that their war-time partnership with the Workers' and Peasants' State was a full and unqualified one. In it, Roosevelt and Churchill jointly proclaimed their acceptance of the concept of the peaceful co-existence of the socialist and capitalist states in peace as well as in war. "We express our determination that our nations shall work together in the war and in the peace that will follow."

Even today, when the United States and British imperialists have completely repudiated their pledges and are pursuing policies exactly opposite to those that they promised, the historic significance of the Teheran Declaration remains unimpaired. It marked the end of the period in which the governments of the great imperialist states pretended to ignore the socialist state and to decide world policies as though it were a passing phenomenon. Churchill's betrayal of the spirit of his

188

wartime pledges and Truman's reversal of the policies established by the late President Roosevelt have not altered that historic fact nor reversed the trend. From the publication of the Teheran Declaration until today, the inherent superiority of the socialist system has compelled steadily increasing recognition in every capitalist country and increasing respect on a world scale, despite the war provocations of United States imperialism.

The Teheran Declaration proclaimed agreement between the big three upon over-all plans for military victory and to "banish the scourge and the terror of war for many generations."[1] The Labor-Progressive Party declared "The agreement arrived at in the Teheran conference is important to all mankind because it provides the sole basis upon which complete democratic victory can be achieved and a just and lasting peace established."[2] Against the opposition of the Tories, of the clerical fascists masquerading as Liberals, and of the C.C.F. leadership, the L.P.P. emphasized that "The reason why those promises were made in the Teheran Declaration is because the world, and the relationship of forces throughout the world, have changed."[3] The party warned the working people:

> "Whether it is fully carried out depends entirely upon the strength and unity of the movement for democratic progress throughout the world. Something has been gained the like of which never has been gained before. The task of democratic people all over the world is to build up and unite their forces and make sure that the high promise in the pledge will be carried out."[4]

The tremendous victories then being achieved by the Red Army over the flower of Hitler's Wehrmacht and the fact that the leaders of the United Nations alliance were agreed upon their over-all strategy found reflection in the rapid spread of public discussion of post-war problems and proposals. In Canada as in Britain and the United States, powerful sections of monopoly-capital and its fascist hangers-on were already planning what they described as "the right war" which they hoped would follow victory in the people's war. Powerful financial interests in Canada were seeking closer relationships with United States imperialism, with the aim of gaining direct imperialist advantages out of the war. The jingoistic, anti-foreign and particularly anti-Soviet diatribes that appeared in sections of the capitalist press, French and English, illustrated the organized character of the capitalist campaign against the growing sense of unity between the peoples of Canada and the Soviet Union. The leaders of the C.C.F. made matters easy for the reactionary forces by noisy and pretentious but completely irresponsible speeches on the theme of "Socialism Now" and declarations that they would establish "socialist planning" after the first post-war election. All over the country, C.C.F. spokesmen, most of whom knew very little about the labor movement and even less about the economic laws of motion of capitalist society, were indulging in silly, hair-raising "prophecies" about what they pretended was going to happen when the fighting stopped. As part of their narrow and purely self-seeking electoral aims, they claimed that mass unemployment, widespread bankruptcies and evictions, economic chaos, in fact, would follow right on the heels of the war "unless the people elected a C.C.F. government.

The L.P.P. concentrated its main fire against the openly reactionary aims of the Tories. Pointing out the character of post-war policies would be determined to a very great extent by the degree of unity achieved by the democratic forces in the winning of the war, the L.P.P. called upon the working-class movement to defeat Tory attempts at division by strengthening "national unity to win the war." The party systematically reminded Canadian workers that men who had favored military cooperation with Hitler Germany before the war and during its early stages, such as George Drew, and provincial governments which had been willing to grant the Nazis a Canadian base of operations in the Gulf of St. Lawrence, such as the Duplessis government, could be defeated only if the majority of people were united for victory and democratic advance. The L.P.P. opposed the demoralizing confusion being spread by the C.C.F. spokesmen.

The C.C.F. propaganda about "Socialism Now" contradicted the objective conditions prevailing in Canada and, as the party emphasized, it misrepresented the limited political aims of the great majority of Canadian workers. Communists fought for a working-class approach to the problems of the post-war period based upon economic and political realities. The L.P.P. emphasized as always that socialism would enable the masses of Canadians to produce a great deal more, enjoy a vastly higher standard of life and richer, more fruitful leisure than is possible under capitalism. But, the party emphasized also, with only a very small minority of Canadian workers as yet in favor of the abolition of capitalism, honest, realistic working-class leadership must concentrate upon issues and aims the struggle for which will move the whole working class forward. The L.P.P. appealed to the national leadership of the C.C.F. to recognize that the immediate issue of post-war national policy and therefore of the then pending federal election, would be "democratic progress through the peaceful co-existence of the capitalist and socialist states," or "imperialist reaction and a drive to a third world war." The party appealed to the C.C.F. as a whole to recognize that, in the conditions then prevailing in Canada baseless declarations that the only alternative to post-war policies of capitalist reaction would be "socialist planning by a C.C.F. government," could only divide the forces that should be united in the struggle for democratic progress.

The claim has been made that the party's opposition to C.C.F. "Socialism Now" propaganda and its emphasis upon parliamentary action at that time were expressions of Browderism in the L.P.P. That claim is unjustified as a study of party reports and resolutions shows.

It is undeniable that the L.P.P. became infected by some of the propaganda of Browderism; because a very substantial number of party members read more of the U.S. party's publications at that time than of our own and then as now the prestige of our brother party was very high in Canada. In addition it must be remembered that the late President Roosevelt was then playing an outstanding role. An example of how our party was influenced by the propaganda from across the line was illustrated by a comrade during the national conference in August, 1945. Then, speaking in the debate on the manner in which Browderism had infected our party, that delegate said: "I must admit that, anytime I, was in doubt, I followed the line of the *Daily Worker* in preference to the line of our own national leadership." That attitude was all too common.

Our opposition to the "Socialism Now" propaganda of the C.C.F., our energetic advocacy of a national front, our emphasis upon the importance of parliamentary action, were not expressions of Browderism. Those comrades who tended to equate such activities with Browderism revealed thereby their own ignorance of what that anti-Marxist current was.

Like the "American Exceptionalism" in an earlier period, Browderism was an attempt to relegate the Communist movement to a role that a section of the bourgeoisie wanted it to play. It attempted to rationalize its betrayal by propagating an anti-Marxist, petty-bourgeois "theory" that the United States capitalists, guided by "their own intelligent self-interest," would work with the progressive forces to maintain friendly relationships and economic cooperation with the socialist countries after the war. It fostered the idea that United States imperialism would cease to be predatory and would seek instead to cooperate in helping the colonial peoples to establish their national sovereignty, industrialize their countries and abolish inequalities between themselves and the western nations. Like the American Exceptionalists, Browder sought to protect his system of petty-bourgeois ideas from Marxist criticism by proclaiming them to be so new that understanding of them could not be found "in the old- books" of Marxism-Leninism. The outstanding expression of Browderisin was the dissolution of the Communist Party of the United States and its replacement by an educational association on the ground that "the new situation" had rendered a Communist party unnecessary and an obstacle to progress.

The Labor-Progressive Party did not advocate or support any of those anti-Marxist ideas. Following the decision of the Central Committee of the C.P. of the U.S.A. to dissolve, the National Committee of the L.P.P. rejected a proposal to take the same action in Canada. Against the delusion that intelligent capitalists would lead the capitalists as a class along the path of post-war cooperation with the Soviet Union and the People's Democracies, the National Committee of the L.P.P. warned Canadian workers that: "There is a grouping of powerful interests seeking to secure control of Canada so as to get back to policies similar to those which prevailed before the war."[5] The party called upon its members to unite the working class against the monopolists, "The enemies of post-war cooperation."

But the party's leadership saw in the gains made during the period of the National Front an important stage in the development of a conscious and systematic struggle by the working class for the leadership of the nation.

To help maintain the political advance then being made by the working class, to strengthen the forces fighting for socialism, to keep open the path to a socialist Canada, it was necessary that all progressive forces in Canadian politics should unite upon immediate aims which could command the support of the majority of workers and poor farmers, including important circles of those who were not then prepared to vote for the abolition of capitalism. Indeed, as the party emphasized continually, they must be immediate aims which could command the support of wide circles of democratic people who were not even prepared to vote for the deliberately deceptive doubletalk of the C.C.F. about "Socialism Now."

The L.P.P. did not minimize the magnitude of the problems confronting Canadian democrats. It stated repeatedly that the basic issue confronting us and all mankind was in effect

"The building of a new world or a drive towards a new world war."[6] The monopoly-capitalists and their political henchmen were bent upon getting our country onto the path of preparations for a third world war. The only means by which the pending federal elections could help to defeat their sinister aims was by the election of a government representative of the democratic, forward-looking majority of Canadians; a government which would keep Canada on the path of peace, friendship with the socialist countries, all-round economic development of our own country and advanced social reforms. Did there exist a possibility to elect such a government? The L.P.P. said "Yes, provided that the electoral strength of all democratic forces favoring such policies were united and the King Liberals were made dependent upon the support of a progressive bloc in the new House of Commons."

Six parties were contesting the federal election.[7] The public opinion polls credited the Liberal Party with receiving the support of 30 per cent of the voters and the Progressive-Conservatives the support of 29 per cent. It was considered extremely unlikely that any one party could secure a majority of the popular vote or win a majority of the seats. There was widespread recognition of the probability that the government which took office following the election would be a coalition government. The main aim of the capitalist press and leaders of capitalist parties was to prevent the establishment of a government based upon the type of coalition advocated by the L.P.P. The Tories and the right-wing Liberals counted quite openly upon being able to elect enough members to establish a right-wing Tory-Liberal coalition. The leadership of the C.C.F. publicly welcomed that prospect because a Liberal-Tory coalition government would make them the official opposition. The Labor-Progressive Party campaigned against that shortsighted attitude. It was clear then to an objective student, just as it is clear now in the light of events, that the L.P.P. was correct in its estimation that "Labor, alone, cannot carry through the policies that will be necessary in the post-war years and capital, alone, will not carry through such policies."[8]

"Our proposal, therefore, is that the labor movement (trade union, labor political parties and other working-class organizations) should unite their forces to elect the largest possible number of members to the next Dominion House of Commons and should enter the elections with the declared aim of electing a government representing a Liberal-Labor coalition."[9]

Pointing out that a Liberal-Tory coalition government would mean national policies of Tory reaction, the L.P.P. appealed for unity to prevent such a disaster for Canadian democracy. The aim of the party's campaign was to capture every possible seat for progress and reduce as much as possible the number of Liberals as well as the number of Tories in the new House of Commons. To enable the progressive forces to win enough seats to enable them to hold the "balance of power" in the new House of Commons, the party called upon all workers, farmers and progressive urban middle-class people to unite in support of one candidate in each constituency. The L.P.P. pointed out that such unity would win for the progressive bloc a large number of seats that often are captured by the Liberals with a minority vote. The actual results of the election showed that we had been correct in that estimation.

The main aims of the party in the federal election in June, 1945, were stated in its program as follows:

"The Labor-Progressive Party, as a vital. force in Canadian democracy, enters the coming Dominion election with its own platform and candidates. The L.P.P. believes that national unity can be best expressed in parliament through a coalition of all democratic forces, including the Labor-Progressive Party, the C.C.F., the trade unions, the farmers' movements, and progressive Liberals of town and rural districts. Together, these represent the overwhelming majority of Canadians. Together they can give the necessary leadership, not surrendering their identities but realizing their common aim, prosperity and enduring peace. "Only such a democratic coalition, only such a national unity parliament and government, can lead Canada forward to that new era of national greatness which is now within our reach."(10)

We did not succeed in bringing about an electoral coalition of all democratic forces. Blinded to the real interests of Canadian democracy by their shortsighted desire to be the official opposition to a Liberal-Tory coalition, the leaders of the C.C.F. denounced the L.P.P. proposal violently and fought against it in the trade union movement and the farm organizations. As a result, the outcome of the election was the return of the King Liberals to power, on the basis of a minority of the popular vote.

In accord with the letter and the spirit of our proposals for a united front of progressive forces, the L.P.P. contested only 67 seats. The fact that in that one-quarter of the constituencies 110,000 Canadians cast their votes for the L.P.P. program in spite of the fact that no coalition could be achieved, testified to the existence of a powerful body of democratic opinion. Canadian workers will yet achieve a great people's coalition for a lasting peace and social progress.

Note

1. From the Teheran Declaration.

2. *Unity or Chaos* by Tim Buck, p. 9.

3. *Unity or Chaos,* by Tim Buck, p. 9.

4. *Unity or Chaos,* by Tim Buck, p. 11.

5. Report adopted by the National Committee, L.P.P., Feb., 12, 1944. Published under the title: Canada's Choice, Unity or Chaos.

6. *Unity or Chaos* by Tim Buck, p. 13.

7. Liberals, Progressive-Conservatives, C.C.F., Labor-

Progressive, Social Credit, Bloc Populaire.

8. *What Kind of Government,* p. 10.

9. *What Kind of Government,* p. 10.

10. *Dominion Election Program of the L.P.P., 1945,* p. 7.

CHAPTER EIGHTEEN: Keep Canada Independent

VICTORY WAS ACHIEVED in Europe a month before Canadians voted in the federal election. Japan capitulated two months after the federal election. The cheers at the victory celebrations had scarcely died away before the public attitude of the government towards post-war problems changed. All too soon, the warning uttered at the foundation convention of the party was proven true. On October 27, 1945, less than three months after the Japanese capitulation, President Truman delivered a foreign policy speech at New York on Navy Day. In that speech he discarded all the democratic concepts expressed in his revered predecessor's wartime undertakings. Franklin D. Roosevelt had placed first the need for international cooperation in the spirit of the Teheran and Yalta accords. Roosevelt had hinged his main policies to that. President Truman, delivering his first major speech to the people of the Americas, betrayed his fear about public reaction to his sudden reversal of the Roosevelt policies so soon after he himself, Truman, had affirmed in the Potsdam Treaty his intention to adhere to them. He tried to bridge the gap between his solemn pledges at Potsdam in August and his implicit repudiation of them in October by the lame excuse that "after past ways, the unity among allies, forged by their common peril, has tended to wear out as the danger passed." With that cynical excuse, he ditched the Roosevelt thesis and put in first place his declared determination to use all the power of the government to enable United States imperialism to dominate the post-war world and organize it in its own image. President Truman was joined in that aim a few days later by Mackenzie King of Canada and Clement Attlee, the "labor" prime minister of Britain. From Washington, these three issued a joint statement announcing in very thinly veiled language their decision to scrap the Big Three unity which had provided the key to victory in the war, and to replace it by a U.S.-British-Canadian bloc. Their statement was couched in terms of the atomic bomb but they made it clear that it referred to the whole field of international relations. They discarded the great-power cooperation built up during the war. In place of cooperation they adopted the technique of "atomic diplomacy."

Less than three months after the capitulation of Japanese imperialism these three men started playing with the dangerous idea that the material power of the United States and what they imagined was going to be its monopoly of the atomic bomb would enable them to destroy the People's Democratic governments and restore the old order of things. It revealed their intention to preserve their system of colonial exploitation and oppression, contrary to their solemn pledges in their Atlantic Charter. Instead of helping all peoples to free themselves from exploitation, and to govern their own countries as they chose, they were planning already to re-establish their imperialist grip. The U.S.-British-Canadian "Atomic Bomb Declaration" showed acceptance by the British imperialists of United States domination. Churchill's infamous call to prepare for war against the Soviet Union followed. It was his first public bid for an arrangement by which he and his imperialist associates in Britain might preserve their personal fortunes and class privileges, by selling out the British Empire to United States imperialism. Mackenzie King's intimate participation illustrated the fact that Canadian imperialists shared those alms.

The second convention of the L.P.P., held June 1-5, 1946, warned the Canadian people against the scheme to integrate Canada in the gathering drive of American imperialism to a third world war. The main resolution adopted by that convention pointed out:

"World peace and reconstruction are in serious danger. The ruthless, imperialistic atomic bomb power politics of the Anglo-American bloc have brought about a tense and critical world situation. An unprecedented campaign of misrepresentation, slander and outright lies has been launched to make it appear that the Soviet Union threatens the peace of the world, to mask the warlike plans of the Anglo-American bloc, and to ideologically prepare the people of Canada for war in the near future, a war for Anglo-American imperialist world domination. "Their drive to make Canada a cockpit of world war three would bring about the subjugation of our country and its democratic institutions to a foreign, imperialist military system-the triumph of North American fascism. "This grim prospect, which would mean devastation and ruin for our country, is not inevitable. To avert it requires that Canadians grasp now all the implications of the deep-going conflict that is under way between the forces of peace and those who are striving for war."[1]

There were honest progressive-minded workers at that time who thought the L.P.P. convention exaggerated the danger of war. Some thought that we exaggerated the treachery of the Canadian monopolists and their political representatives. Not one such worker thinks so today.

In accord with Truman's emphasis on the new aims of American imperialism in his Navy Day speech, the head of the State Department's policy planning division, George F. Kennan, elaborated a vicious, far-reaching, war-mongering Nazi, argument to the effect that the main point of United States foreign policy should be directed against the Soviet Union, instead of to cooperation on the basis of the United Nations Charter for world peace. In March, 1947, President Truman made another foreign policy speech and proclaimed his "get-tough-with-Russia" policy, under the official title of "The Truman Doctrine." His proclamation was in fact but the public announcement that his administration had adopted the vicious, anti-democratic Kennan plan as the basis of its official foreign policy.

The over-all aim of the Truman Doctrine and the

supplementary policies which have been introduced to buttress it, such as the Marshall Plan, etc., is United States domination of the world. As Lenin pointed out, imperialism is characterized everywhere by a striving for complete domination. In this epoch of the crisis of the imperialist system and the transition to socialism, the drive for imperialist domination is not concentrated solely, or even mainly, upon the so-called "undeveloped" colonial countries. Now, the imperialists are motivated by military considerations even more strongly than by potential superprofits to be secured through domination of "undeveloped" countries. In addition, the U.S. imperialists find that dominating and exploiting the people of an industrially developed country by making its capitalists dependent upon U.S. "aid" is also very profitable to Wall Street. Thus, the U.S. drive for domination is directed first of all at other imperialist states - Canada, Britain, France, Italy, Western Germany, etc. It is carried on in the disguise of the search for security, in the disguise of Marshall Plan aid, arms aid, economic cooperation, or what have you. Its aim, and until now, its result, is consistently the same. The Yankee moneybags are seeking to dominate and exploit the rest of mankind, as well as to involve them in a world atomic war for U.S. aggrandizement.

President Truman's declaration in March, 1947, that his government puts the maintenance of capitalism before and above the maintenance of peace, was a veiled public assurance to United States monopoly-capital that, henceforth, all the resources of American imperialism would be used to stop the popular democratic advance which at that time characterized the old world. His government was already pursuing an aggressive and provocative war policy. In that very speech he proposed that the United States should transform Greece and Turkey into military and naval bases for United States imperialism "to stop the spread of communism." As the Labor-Progressive Party pointed out at the time, the Truman Doctrine speech "was the most flagrant admission of aggressive, imperialist intent that has been made since Hitler proclaimed *his* aggressive aims before the Second

World War. Never before in the memory of any man living has the responsible head of a great power proclaimed brazenly and arrogantly his aim at world domination and the intent to achieve it by flagrant interference in the internal affairs of other nations."

Following the president's "Truman Doctrine" speech, the Marshall Plan was introduced as its economic counterpart. Promptly the St. Laurent government changed the entire basis of Canada's foreign trade policies to make them conform with the sinister aims of the Truman Doctrine and its Marshall Plan. The first, and drastic, change in Canadian foreign trade policies became known as the Abbott Plan. So determined was the St. Laurent government to carry through its changes that it prevented any public knowledge of them, even by parliament, until after they were in operation. For the first time since responsible government was established in Canada, the government of the day introduced basic changes in national policy and foreign relationships in peacetime by simply announcing the changes over the radio. Relatively few people understood from Douglas Abbott's misleading broadcast that the whole emphasis of Canadian relationships, economic and political, was being changed; that "the British connection" was being ditched. That makes the method used by the St. Laurent government more reprehensible.

It became quite clear that Canadian imperialists were bent upon making themselves junior partners of the United States imperialists at the expense of the Canadian people. They cynically discarded the national ambition that Sir Wilfrid Laurier used to describe in his boast, "This will be Canada's century." Instead of developing Canada's economy, they adopted the aim of becoming political as well as financial "brokers," seizing options on political, economic, territorial and military advantages in Canada for the U.S. imperialists, literally selling Canada to the United States. Along with that aim and function, there developed rapidly one project after another by which United States authority within Canada increased, and Canada's sovereignty was systematically undermined.

The Labor-Progressive Party called upon the Canadian people to recognize that the Abbott Plan was a great deal more than a temporary expedient as the government pretended. It was clearly the beginning of a long-range scheme to subordinate Canada's economy and trade policies to the United States. It has already subordinated Canada's export trade to the United States government. To maintain Canada as an outlet for U.S. manufacturers, it has blocked the expansion of finished goods industries. It is making Canada dependent upon the production of raw materials for U.S. industries. It has disrupted the century-old trade relationships between Canada and Britain. It has cut off Canadian exporters from trade with nearly half of all mankind. It is forcing a generation of young Canadians to emigrate to the United States in search of careers. It has granted U.S. troops extra-territorial rights in Canada, reduced parts of our country to "U.S.-occupied territory." These are but the early fruits of the St. Laurent aims, which started with the Abbott Plan. It was the concrete form of the policy by which the Canadian representatives of international finance-capital, personified by the Right Honorable Louis St. Laurent, planned a gigantic auction-the sale of our national birthright.

To every Marxist it was clear in December, 1947, that if the Abbott Plan should be carried through to its logical conclusion, our power to decide upon any question of domestic or international relationships, our national sovereignty, even the national survival of the two peoples of Canada, would be jeopardized. The L.P.P. called upon the working-class movement to reject the Abbott Plan, to reject the aims represented by the then minister for external affairs, St. Laurent. The party called upon the working class to "Keep Canada Independent!"

But, argued some progressive-minded people, "That is bourgeois nationalism!"

The charge could not be brushed off but at the same time

the long-range aims of the St. Laurent government had to be exposed and combatted if the path was to be kept open for the eventual victory of people's democracy and the achievement of socialism in Canada. It led to study by the party leadership of the role of the working class in the nation. The study showed clearly that the role of the working, class in the struggle for the national interests has advanced tremendously. As a consequence of the profound and increasingly evident contradiction between the predatory aims and policies of monopoly-capital and the interests of the overwhelming majority of the people, the real nation, the relationship of the working-class movement to "the national interests" has changed. It is wrong today to suggest that "the national interests" in Canada are solely the "business" of the capitalist class. It is true that Canada is an imperialist state, dominated by monopolistic finance-capital and the tightly-knit oligarchy which directs the affairs of the monopolies which, octopus-like, suck the life-blood from every section of the working people. It is true that the ambitions of the narrow clique of unscrupulous men who direct the affairs of monopoly-capital determine the present national policies of Canada. But those men are not the Canadian nation. Indeed, excepting that some of them accidentally were born in this country, they are not Canadians. Their interests and predatory ambitions are anti-Canadian.

Now the battle for Canadian independence does have to be fought again, but against a new form of servitude. Our struggle today is different from that of the colonial peoples, fighting against national enslavement imposed upon them by the armed forces of foreign imperialists. We are threatened with complete national enslavement to a foreign power, but that power is not, at least not yet, imposing its control by the force of arms. Canada is being sold into United States control by "her own" ruling class; the parasitic, speculative, Canadian manipulators of stock market deals, politics and governmental concessions, who are enriching themselves by trading the national future of Canada for junior partnerships in the United States monopolies.

Widening circles of democratic people recognize the deepening contradictions between the real interests of the nation and the aims of the monopolists. Increasing numbers of democratic Canadians are prepared to act in defence of the true national interests, against the treachery of the peace-time Vichyites of Canada, the political servants of international finance-capital. In a monopoly-capitalist state such as Canada is today, democratic struggle to defend the national interests against such treachery can be carried through only to the extent that the working class is drawn into that struggle, and accepts responsibility for its success. The working-class movement can lead that struggle succcessfully only to the extent that it is inspired by an understanding of its own role and responsibility, as the vanguard representative of a historic class which, even to save itself, must lead Canada forward in peaceful association with the half of all mankind who are now carrying through a great, historic, progressive advance. By that path, the working class will win the leadership of the nation. Because that is the path of struggle for the true interests of Canada and its people, against the predatory ambitions of the masters of crisis-stricken imperialism, the Labor-Progressive Party is proud to be called "The Party of the Nation." Our party seeks to lead the majority of Canadians, rallied around the working class, in the struggle to preserve all that is best in our democratic national traditions, to "Keep Canada Independent!" To develop, improve and enrich without limit our wide and rich and lovely land and its people.

Note

1. *For Peace, Progress, Socialism.* Reports and Resolutions, Second National Convention Labor-Progressive Party, pp. 51-52.

CHAPTER NINETEEN: We Fight for Canada!

THE HISTORY of our movement is the history of the struggle for social progress in Canada throughout the past thirty years. Our strivings for social progress at home have been accompanied, always, by unremitting advocacy of national policies to make our country a force for world peace, through fruitful cooperation between the socialist and capitalist countries. Our party has been the most consistent as well as the most energetic champion of French-English unity. Our party initiated and leads the fight to abolish the economic inequalities imposed upon the workers of French Canada and to win for its people the right of national self-determination. Our movement has won recognition as the sole defender of the true interests of Canada's youth and the most consistent organizer of the women of Canada, to strengthen and extend their role in the shaping of public policies and to defend their interests-as workers and as women. Throughout our three decades of activity the Communist movement has been in the forefront of all the struggles to defend the real interests of the farmers and of the urban middle-class people. Above all, our movement has been the embodiment of the struggle to extend trade union organization, to develop and strengthen understanding of the need for industrial unionism, to develop labor unity, to deepen and extend the consciousness of the workers of their interests and their historic mission as a class.

The battle for unity and class consciousness is the essence of the historical development of the working class. Class consciousness and united action are the keys to working-class leadership of the nation. The Labor-Progressive Party is the party which, guided by Marxist-Leninist science, fights for the steadily rising level of political historical understanding which enables the progressive elements to be a unifying and guiding force in the working-class movement.

* * *

The main content of our struggles has been constant throughout our history but their form has changed from time to time with changing conditions. The most marked of all such changes was brought about by the great democratic advances achieved in numerous countries following the People's War. The People's War of Liberation changed the world. Through struggle and victory over fascism, 600 million people put an end to the dictatorship of the landlords and foreign bankers in their countries, and established People's Democratic governments. People's Democracy and the amazing achievements of socialist economy and socialist science in the Soviet Union have transformed the prospects for world development. In the Soviet Union and the People's Democracies 800 million people, a third of all mankind, are now united in the building of a new, higher, immeasurably more democratic society-socialism. As a result of their historic advance, the crucial, immediately decisive question of world politics is now that of the relationship between the capitalist and the socialist sectors of the world.

The change is continuing. Teeming millions of awakening people in all the lands that previously were referred to as colonies are demanding national independence, the right to govern themselves in their own way. In country after country: Burma, India, Indonesia, etc., etc., the imperialists have been compelled to concede varying degrees of self-government. The people's struggles for national independence and the democratic upsurge of popular enthusiasm in the building of socialism in the Soviet Union and the People's 'Democracies cannot be defeated. Historically they are irresistible because they are the personal as well as the collective aims of hundreds of millions of people. This typifies one of the most profound and far-reaching changes that accompanied the people's victory over fascism. The masses of the people have always been involved in great social conflicts, particularly in modern times. Hitherto the masses of the people have been involved as pawns, ignorant of the real aims for which they sacrificed and died. Today, however, the masses of the people are becoming conscious participants in great social struggles to achieve aims that they set themselves.

In Canada and all the imperialist countries the deepening crisis of the imperialist system is bringing the masses of the people face to face with the supreme issue of our age. Two alternatives confront Canadians today. The democratic choice is acceptance of the new state of things. That choice includes acceptance of the idea and the aim of the peaceful coexistence of the socialist and capitalist countries. It includes the prospect of literally unlimited trade between the socialist and capitalist countries, democratic cooperation in -bringing about a great, world-wide transformation - the abolition of poverty and way.

The other, the anti-democratic alternative, is blind refusal to accept the verdict of history, to choose instead to continue support of the international clique of financiers who, under the leadership of the United States monopolists, are trying to launch a world atomic war in the madman's hope that it might be possible by that means to re-establish the old order of things.

Now the imperialists seek way not *only* to extend their domination. The Canadian imperialists even surrender their own sovereignty and accept United States domination as part of their striving to make themselves partners in United States war preparations. In their insensate hatred of socialism and their greed for quick and easy profits they are not only enslaving Canada to the United States, they are undermining the democratic rights of all Canadians, cultivating the elements of fascism, the accompaniment of predatory imperialist war. The alternatives *they* prefer are imperialist domination of the world or the destruction of civilization.

Continued support of the imperialists would mean national policies aimed to foster official Canadian hostility toward the people of the Soviet Union and the People's

Democracies. It would mean continued subordination of all questions concerning Canada's welfare to United States plans for war. It would mean continued and ever-increasing sacrifice of Canada's civilian economy to the growing state-monopoly-capitalist war economy, with its inflation, soaring prices of consumer goods, higher and higher taxes upon small incomes for the cynical purpose of reducing civilian consumption. It would continue to create chronic and growing mass unemployment until, because of the impossibility of continuing further, either the imperialists succeed in launching the war for which they are preparing, or the armaments burden brings down the economic structure in a crash which will make the crisis of 1929 look like a "recession."

In this situation the L.P.P. takes its stand unequivocally in the great democratic camp of struggle for peace. Peace is the vital need of Canada. Provided peace is maintained, Canadians can set their sights on a great new era of economic development, rising living standards, and democratic advance in our country. Peace is the vital need of the overwhelming majority of all mankind. The peoples of the Soviet Union and the People's Democracies want peace. They want to build their new social order, to abolish poverty and backwardness from their lands forever. Democratic men and women in all imperialist countries want peace; they know that an imperialist world war could have no purpose other than to set the clock back at home as well as abroad.

The maintenance of peace will keep the path open for continued social progress, for the eventual achievement of socialism in Canada; while an atomic world war would probably bring about the end of civilization. Because of that, the L.P.P. subordinates all other questions to the vital need to mobilize all the forces of Canadian democracy to stop the insane drive to war. The Canadian people can defeat the underhanded conspiracy to transform our country to a United States colony, a depressed raw-material hinterland for the U.S. monopolies, a training ground for U.S. troops, only by making the will to peace supreme in Canada.

209

As the party's third national convention pointed out in February" 1949:

"All the efforts of monopoly capital to extricate the system from crisis by instigating world war at the expense of the peoples can and must be defeated by united resistance., Forceful demands must be raised by labor for world diplomatic cooperation, new policies of world trade and freedom from U.S. domination. Canadian democratic policy must recognize the inescapable fact that imperialism is declining, that the socialist and new democratic world is here to stay, and that Canada must fit in with the new world which arose out of the defeat of the Axis powers."[1]

To those who question the possibility of preventing imperialist war, of preventing imperialist governments from resorting to war, the Communist answer is that, given a sufficient degree of working-class unity and leadership, the defenders of peace can prevent a third world war precisely because of the changes which now impel the imperialists to look to war as their last desperate resort. In Canada, the United States, Britain, France, Italy, in all imperialist countries, as well as in the colonial lands, the unconscious involvement of the masses of the people in struggles to achieve the predatory ambitions of the capitalist class is being supplanted by the conscious participation of millions of democratic people in actions to prevent a third world war. As a result there has arisen a mighty organized world movement unprecedented in history. It unites all defenders of peace without regard to differing ideologies or differing opinions as to the source of the danger of war. It demands an end to war propaganda, a pact of peace between the five great powers-U.S., Soviet Union, Britain, France and People's China. It demands disarmament, the banning of atomic weapons and respect for the sovereign rights of all nations. The magnitude of the democratic actions already developed against the U.S. drive for war is illustrated by the fact that 600 million people, spread over literally every part of the world, have signed the demand that the five great powers sign a mutual pact of peace. This great democratic world movement is as yet in its early stages but already it is supported by as many adults as all the adults there are in all the countries which support United States war policies in the United Nations Organization.

The will of the people will prevail in the struggle for peace. The people defeated the plans of the Rome-Berlin-Tokyo fascist axis for world conquest; they will defeat the plans of the United States imperialists also-the difference is that now millions of democratic people are realizing that they can best defeat the warmongers, and to the best advantage of mankind, by preventing them from launching another world war.

In the struggle to maintain peace the working class will achieve its class unity. The workers achieved industrial unionism in the face of every obstacle that the capitalist class and its labor lieutenants could put in the way; now, at this higher stage of political struggle, they will achieve their class unity also. Democratic Canadians defeated Bennett's "Iron Heel" policies and forced the repeal of Section 98. In their battle now against the drive to war, they will stop the systematic attacks upon civil rights, compel the repeal of such fascist laws as the Padlock Law in the province of Quebec and the "Garson Amendments," and defeat the attempt to smuggle fascism into Canada. Defeating the warmongers and their political servants, particularly the right-wing social-democrats, the working class will win its ideological independence from the capitalist class. As the masses of the people freed themselves from the obscurantism and political passivity of feudalism through their participation in the struggles of the bourgeoisie, so now the workers will free themselves from ideological enslavement to the bourgeoisie as they fight for their shining ideal of People's Democracy, Peace and Socialism; against the imperialists' drive to war. Through these struggles the working class will win the moral and political leadership of the nation.

* * *

The basic aim of all our activities is to help the working class to accomplish the tasks indicated above. We urge all democratic Canadians to demand that Canadian governments, federal and provincial, publicly advocate "peace by negotiation," and repudiate the United States slogan "peace through strength," which is in fact the path to war. We fight to win broad, popular support for the idea of "the peaceful co-existence of the socialist and capitalist systems." We declare unequivocally that our economic well-being, our national security, the independence of Canada, all depend upon the peaceful co-existence of the capitalist and socialist countries on the basis of respect for national rights and independence.

We fight for trade between Canada and all countries which desire to buy Canadian products or have products that we need. We fight for the outright prohibition of all atomic weapons, destruction of all stocks of atomic weapons under strict international inspection and control, and continued systematic international inspection under the, authority of the United Nations to ensure that no more are produced. We advocate step-by-step reduction of armaments, under United Nations control, on a scale and in a manner consistent with the national security of Canada and all countries.

The Labor-Progressive Party is the party of the working class, of socialism. In Canada as in all capitalist countries, the sole means by' which socialism can be achieved is the political victory of the united forces of the democratic people, led by the working class. There is no contradiction whatsoever between our loyal, unconditional participation in the movement to avert war now, a movement which does not challenge the profit system, and our ultimate objective of abolishing war forever by abolishing the profit system. Far from being contradictory, attainment of the immediate objective of preserving peace is a necessary requisite to the attainment of our ultimate ideal. Furthermore, the path to our ideal is the only path by which Canadian democracy can flourish.

The Canadian people can maintain civil rights, democratic progress, their living standards, the independence of Canada, and extend social reforms, only by consistent all-sided struggle against the monopolists and their political agents who are seeking to subvert democracy. The advance towards socialism in Canada can be made only by the same path-all-sided militant defence of peace and democracy. Economically our country is ripe for socialism. All the possibilities inherent within the profit system have been developed; it has become now a barrier to continued Canadian development on a rising level to the full capacity of our abundantly endowed country and our productive people. Through its inherent contradictions which are now acute, the profit system leads to economic crisis and imperialist war. For the working class the only permanent solution of these contradictions is through the struggle to raise themselves up from the position of an oppressed and exploited class to the position of the ruling class, and the abolition of the profit system.

Socialism means freedom. Freedom from poverty, insecurity, exploitation and war. It means the full flowering of individual, spirit and initiative. It will provide, for the first time in Canada, opportunities to develop the full potential of every human being. It means the freeing of women from the inequalities imposed upon them by capitalism with its sanctification of relationships of dependence and sex superiority. Socialism will give to women, for the first time, completely equal rights with men in all branches of the social, economic and political life of Canada. Socialism will open up new opportunities both in preparation for and fulfillment of careers for Canada's youth. It will guarantee the full development and conservation of our land, and a more secure, a richer and happier life for every family in it.

Capitalist spokesmen and their agents within the labor movement foster the lie that the Communists aim to destroy Parliament. For them that lie is a necessary element in their "Big

Lie," that Communists aim to subordinate the interests of Canada to the interests of the Soviet Union. That is patterned directly upon Hitler's technique. It is the opposite of the truth. Canadian Communists *fight for Canada!* We have declared categorically scores of times: in our program, our conventions, our public documents, etc., that our alms do not include the abolition of Parliament or of the parliamentary form of government. Indeed, if the hired propagandists of monopoly-capital made any effort to be consistent, they would recognize that the people of Canada can advance to socialism utilizing the parliamentary form of government equally as the workers and farmers of the countries of Central and Southeastern Europe did.

Candians will achieve socialism by their own path, which will be determined by the traditions and the then prevailing institutions and class relationships in Canada. It is quite evident, however, that the socialist transformation of our country can be achieved only if the working class and its allies gain real political power. To establish socialism, the state must become an instrument in the hands of the democratic people united around and led by the working class. It must be an instrument of the people for the organization, direction and defence of the new socialist society, instead of, as it is now, the instrument by which the capitalist class maintains its heartless exploitation of the masses of the people and its ruthless suppression of their democratic aspirations. To accomplish that change it is necessary to build a great alliance of democratic forces around a broad, democratic, forward-looking People's Program, and develop a tremendous movement of the united working-class and democratic farm and urban middle-class people to carry it through. That is decisive. The Labor-Progressive Party declares that Canadian workers and their allies can win real political power, take it out of the hands of the parties of monopoly-capitalism, provided that the masses of progressive-minded people are rallied around the working class in a broad alliance of democratic forces: Communists, social reformers, trade unions, farm organizations, French- and English-speaking, Catholics and Protestants. That is the form in which the democratic masses of Canadians can defeat the political parties of monopoly-capital; eventually they will.

The working class cannot establish socialism by simple electoral victory, but the parliamentary victory of such a broad alliance of democratic forces can transform capitalist democracy into real people's democracy and make Parliament, which has developed as a result of the traditions and democratic struggles of the Canadian people, into an instrument of People's Democracy-the instrument through which the democratic people, led by the working class, make their will supreme.

Through the victory of People's Democracy real power will be transferred from the hands of the numerically small clique of monopolists who direct the affairs of finance-capital and its stranglehold on the national economy, to the hands of the overwhelming majority of the people, headed by the working class. The People's Democratic government will carry into effect the socialist nationalization of the key industries, the banks and the credit system; the commanding heights of the national economy. It will re-establish Canada's independence, freeing us from the present subservience to the United States. People's Democracy will make Canada a positive force for peace in the United Nations Organization.

* * *

In every struggle of the day for the immediate interests of the working class, the Labor-Progressive Party brings forward the idea of its goal, "A People's Democratic Government." That will be our first, decisive step for the establishment of lasting peace and the winning through to a socialist Canada. The L.P.P. devotes all its efforts to winning the majority of the Canadian working class, and progressive farm and urban middle-class people, for the fulfillment of this program. The record of our work through the past thirty years is proof both of our sincerity and the

215

certainty of final victory.

Guided by the science of Marxism-Leninism and the inspiring examples of the working people of the Soviet Union and the People's Democratic Republics, the Canadian working class will replace the profit system, and its soulless exploitation of man by man, by a social system in which, because of its collective ownership of all the means of large-scale social production, the free development of each will be the condition for the free development of all. Such is the greater and richer Canada for which we strive-a socialist Canada-contributing freely to and sharing freely in the economic and cultural advance to the now rapidly approaching world triumph of socialism.

We call on all Canadians who want peace, a more abundant life, national independence, friendship with all other peoples, and socialism, to join our ranks: *"Play your part in the fight for a People's Canada by joining Canada's Party of Communists!"*

Note

1. *Main Resolution,* Second National Convention L.P.P., Feb. 4-8, 1949.